SpringerBriefs in Law

SpringerBriefs present concise summaries of cutting-edge research and practical applications across a wide spectrum of fields. Featuring compact volumes of 50 to 125 pages, the series covers a range of content from professional to academic. Typical topics might include:

- A timely report of state-of-the art analytical techniques
- A bridge between new research results, as published in journal articles, and a contextual literature review
- A snapshot of a hot or emerging topic
- A presentation of core concepts that students must understand in order to make independent contributions

SpringerBriefs in Law showcase emerging theory, empirical research, and practical application in Law from a global author community. SpringerBriefs are characterized by fast, global electronic dissemination, standard publishing contracts, standardized manuscript preparation and formatting guidelines, and expedited production schedules.

Fernando Messias

The Practice of Law and International Arbitration in the Age of Artificial Intelligence

Springer

Fernando Messias
Lisbon, Portugal

ISSN 2192-855X ISSN 2192-8568 (electronic)
SpringerBriefs in Law
ISBN 978-3-032-09126-0 ISBN 978-3-032-09127-7 (eBook)
https://doi.org/10.1007/978-3-032-09127-7

This Springer imprint is published by the registered company Springer Nature Switzerland AG.
The registered company address is: Gewerbestrasse 11, 6330 Cham, Switzerland

Foreword 1

The technological evolution we have witnessed over the last three decades has redefined not only the way we interact with the world, but also the paradigms of legal practice and international arbitration.

In my own professional practice, I have gone from the electronic typewriter to the desktop computer powered by floppy disks, witnessed the reign of the fax, the popularisation of Word, the beginnings of email and the vulgarisation of the internet, search engines, smartphones, citius and video conferencing.

Artificial intelligence (AI), only recently considered an element of science fiction, is already an unprecedented leap into the future.

In less than two years it has become an indispensable tool in various sectors, including law, where it is an indispensable resource for optimising processes, boosting efficiency and even democratising access to justice.

This book by Fernando Messias, 'The Practice of Law and International Arbitration in the Age of Artificial Intelligence', comes at a crucial time for understanding the impact and possibilities that AI brings to the legal world.

Over the next few pages, the reader will be guided through an in-depth analysis of how this technology is shaping the practice of law, alternative dispute resolution and international arbitration.

Fernando Messias is a polymath; as well as being a brilliant lawyer, he is a prolific writer, a navigator of the future and an early adopter of Artificial Intelligence.

The discussion presented here goes beyond the mere operational aspects of adopting AI in law. Fernando takes us on a reflective journey that considers the ethical dilemmas, the regulatory implications and the challenges facing professionals in the sector. After all, the inclusion of AI in the practice of law is not just a question of efficiency, but also of preserving fundamental rights, transparency and accountability in decision-making. One of the most sensitive aspects addressed in this book is the balance between human judgment and AI-assisted automation. To what extent can algorithms replace human judgment in decision-making processes? How can we ensure that AI models are trained without biases that jeopardise fairness? How can trust in legal institutions be maintained when decision-making is shared between humans and machines? These are some of the questions that emerge and will be explored in depth. However, coming down to earth and to practical problems, one of the biggest impacts of AI on the practice of law will be its ability to allow real scrutiny of large quantities of documents in complex cases. These days, this exhaustive analysis is, in most cases, an illusion. In many media cases, the Public Prosecutor's Office pompously announces the seizure of terabytes of information and hundreds of thousands of documents, plus many hours of wiretapping. In practice, these documents and bytes will never be analysed in their entirety and the wiretaps will remain unheard. The vastness of the information available far exceeds the human capacity to process it, leading to many relevant elements being simply ignored, creating a false impression that the evidence has been properly scrutinised. AI, with its data processing and pattern recognition capabilities, promises to change this paradigm, ensuring that all evidence is effectively analysed and that judicial decisions can be based on more solid and comprehensive factual knowledge than is the case today. Still in the case of Portugal, one of the biggest obstacles to harnessing the potential of AI lies in the lack of transparency of judicial decisions. There is no access to first instance decisions and, even in the case of higher courts, there is an incomprehensible selection of publicised decisions. Unlike in other countries, there is no access either to the parties' pleadings or to the testimony of witnesses and experts, which prevents a more in-depth analysis of cases and jeopardises the development of AI models applicable to the Portuguese legal system. This opacity not only limits innovation and the efficiency of the justice system, but also slows down the learning of large-scale language models (LLM) in Portuguese from Portugal, hindering the creation of technological tools adapted to our legal reality.

In the field of arbitration and international arbitration, the ability to analyse evidence in different languages and cultural contexts and even to compare legal systems will provide a huge qualitative leap forward. But this revolution has only just begun. It is expected that, by the end of 2025, some of the concepts analysed here will have become obsolete and new frontiers will open up before our eyes. The pace of innovation is overwhelming, and the implications for international law and arbitration will be even more profound than we can foresee today. New challenges will arise, requiring constant adaptation from professionals in the sector, as well as ongoing reflection on the limits and possibilities of AI in the pursuit of justice.

For lawyers, arbitrators, researchers and law students, this book is an invitation to debate and reflect.

Fernando Messias offers us a comprehensive overview of the challenges and opportunities that AI presents for international law and arbitration. More than a portrait of the present, this book looks to the future, pointing out paths and directions for a harmonious coexistence between technology and justice.

I wish readers an enriching journey through the pages that follow, in the hope that this book will inspire reflection and contribute to building a very near future where AI is an ally of justice, rather than a challenge to its essence.

Dr João Valadas Coriel
Lawyer, Managing Partner of VCA, Law Firm,
Valadas Coriel & Associados

Foreword 2

We live in the present dimension: TODAY, although in a nanosecond everything can change. Fernando Messias has managed to bring together in this book a wealth of scientific knowledge, which he conveys to us with an avid collection of data, sources and rapid developments in a world whose evolution is on track to exceed the speed of light. His work addresses the current problems and challenges posed by artificial intelligence in the practice of law and arbitration.

At the Chartered Institute of Arbitrators (CIArb), we are aware of this reality, and I am honoured to write the foreword to Fernando Messias' book in 2025, under the Presidential CIArb year of Mohamed Abdel Wahab, in which, in March, we published the CIArb Guideline on the Use of AI in Arbitration (2025) with the team led by Cristen Bauer and Claire Morel de Westgaver.

In terms of structure, the book is organised into five interconnected chapters. It begins with a General Introduction, which sets the stage by outlining the relationship between Artificial Intelligence and International Arbitration. This is followed by a chapter dedicated to Artificial Intelligence and International Arbitration, exploring topics such as videoconferencing and the principle of immediacy, the integration of AI in law and arbitration, its advantages and challenges, the automation of tasks and evidence management, machine learning, ethics, human judgment, natural language processing, confidentiality, and blockchain applications.

The next chapter, Artificial Intelligence in Law, examines the impact and integration of AI in legal systems, addressing technological advances, operational efficiency and the ethical and practical complexity of algorithmic participation in judicial decision-making.

The following chapter, The Role of AI in Alternative Dispute Resolution (ADR), Advocacy and International Arbitration, analyses the influence of the digital world on communication in arbitration, the cognitive processes of legal professionals and the redefinition of the legal profession in the digital age. It also reviews ADR methods, online dispute resolution (ODR), regulatory aspects such as the UNCITRAL Model Law, the CIArb Guidelines (2025), and European practices, as well as the opportunities and challenges of AI in these processes.

The book concludes with a final epilogue and a general bibliography, which invite reflection on the ethical and legal implications of these technological transformations.

Fernando Messias' vision and mission lead me to join them in the call they made in Rome on 28 February 2020: Call for AI Ethics, a year that marked a new dimension following Charles Darwin in adaptability, evolution, challenges as individuals, as societies and as peoples. Call for AI Ethics is a document signed by the Pontifical Academy for Life, Microsoft, IBM, the United Nations Food and Agriculture Organisation (FAO) and the Italian Ministry of Innovation to promote an ethical approach to artificial intelligence.

Fernando Messias, in his book, conveys, in line with the call for ethics in Artificial Intelligence, the promotion of a sense of shared responsibility among providers, suppliers, in short, the entire legal industry as a pillar through which ordinary jurisdiction and arbitration jurisdiction flow, seeking a coherent future where digital innovation and technological progress give humanity its leading role.

This leading role comes from the algorithms of Artificial Intelligence, like the music that emanates from Nino Rota and Ennio Morricone, from a new algorithmic approach where balance with the Human Being, and I would add Consciousness. May this be the promoter of greater transparency and impartiality by mitigating human bias in search of intellectual honesty.

In short, I hope you enjoy reading this and find new insights into the complex balance between the right of access to justice, the right to judicial secrecy and technological privacy: Technology, law and arbitration in the balance of ethics, education and law through the principles of transparency, inclusion, responsibility, impartiality, reliability, security and privacy. In summary artificial intelligence will be a tool at the service of conscious human beings.

Dr Nazareth Romero
Lawyer, International Arbitrator, FCIArb,
President of the CIArb Iberian Chapter – European Branch of the
Chartered Institute of Arbitrators,
Partner at the Law Firm,
Ovoli Romero Abogados, S.L.

Competing Interests The author has no competing interests to declare that are relevant to the content of this manuscript.

Contents

About the Author

Fernando Messias, LLB, LLM in International Trade Law, PhD in Tourism and Postdoctoral Fellow in Psychology, works as a lawyer, arbitrator and mediator in Portugal and internationally. Specialising in domestic and international arbitration, legal advice in the areas of real estate, industry, tourism and business law, his research focuses on the intersection between Law, Organisational Psychology and Management. Author of multidisciplinary works, he collaborates with companies to optimise organisational performance, applying methods such as Basadur Simplex in the creative resolution of organisational problems.

Foreword's Biographical Note: João Valadas Coriel

João Valadas Coriel is a lawyer. He founded Valadas Coriel, a law firm specialising in Private Clients and Family Offices with a strong international presence. João Valadas Coriel graduated from the Faculty of Law of the University of Lisbon, holds a postgraduate degree in Public Health from the Faculty of Medicine of the New University of Lisbon and a postgraduate degree in Taxation and Business Management from ISEG. He is a member of CIArb – Chartered Institute of Arbitrators, in International Arbitration, a member of the Society of Trust and Estate Practitioners (STEP), and also serves as Vice-Chair of the Senior Lawyers Committee of the International Bar Association and Vice-Chair of the International Private Clients Committee of the American Bar Association.

Foreword's Biographical Note: Nazareth Romero

Nazareth Romero is a lawyer and associate at the law firm Ovoli Romero Abogados, S.L. – Ovoli Frugoni AP, where she is responsible for arbitration and international litigation. She works as an international mediator and arbitrator, as well as President of the ClArb Iberian Chapter – European Branch of the Chartered Institute of Arbitrators — and member of the EU Branch Committee of that Institute. She is a collaborating member of the Royal Academy of Jurisprudence and Legislation of Spain, as well as an external expert at the Directorate-General for Justice and Home Affairs of the European Commission. She is listed as an arbitrator and expert in several international arbitration institutions and international trade bodies. In this regard, she has acted in disputes relating to the EU's bilateral free trade agreements with third countries, as well as in international arbitration proceedings.

Chapter 1
General Introduction

This book addresses Artificial Intelligence (AI) as a tool at the service of Law and International Arbitration, exploring its instrumental reality as a support to human intelligence. The term AI is currently in vogue, with frequent references in the media—whether written (print or digital) or televised. However, despite its popularity, there is still limited knowledge about its concept, scope and practical potential.

AI, as an area of computer science, is dedicated to developing systems capable of performing tasks that traditionally require human intelligence. These include learning, logical reasoning, pattern perception, decision-making and interaction through natural language. This discipline encompasses sub-areas such as machine learning, natural language processing, computer vision and robotics, among others. From a technical perspective, AI is defined as the ability of a computer system to interpret external data, learn from that data and use the knowledge acquired to achieve specific goals, adapting and improving continuously.

The truth is that AI has entered our lives and seems to be a permanent part of them. Whether we like it or not, the reality is that our activities are umbilically linked to the current dynamics of AI. This is first and foremost because it is present in almost everything an individual uses in their daily lives, especially in the labour context. From our mobile phones—where most smartphones employ AI-supported technology for calls, messages, email, web browsing or using apps—to more complex services such as health platforms, financial management, insurance or customer service. Virtual assistants are a clear example of this integration. Google Assistant, developed by Google, stands out for its versatility. Amazon Alexa has become popular due to its voice interaction, making it possible to manage household tasks or play content. Siri, integrated into Apple devices, facilitates actions such as sending messages or searching for information. New tools, such as OpenAI Operator, promise to revolutionise the automation of tasks via the browser, while specific projects, such as Ávoris CAT-AI (developed in partnership with Microsoft and Amadeus), offer personalised solutions for tourists, integrating with platforms

F. Messias, *The Practice of Law and International Arbitration in the Age of Artificial Intelligence*, SpringerBriefs in Law,
https://doi.org/10.1007/978-3-032-09127-7_1

such as WhatsApp. In the area of customer service, W2M MIA 2.0 uses generative AI to improve the customer experience, adapting to each interaction. In mental health, platforms such as Thera Pro AI (available at https://www.therapro.ai) or the 'virtual psychologist' created by Portuguese researchers—a chatbot that simulates psychotherapy appointments—illustrate how AI is transforming even sensitive areas, offering complementary support to professionals and users. From this we can see that, whether it's simplifying routines or innovating in specialised sectors, artificial intelligence has become an irreversible pillar of modern life, shaping not only the present but also the future of human interactions.

With regard to arbitration, the Chartered Institute of Arbitrators recently launched a set of procedures on the use of artificial intelligence in arbitration (Guidelines on the Use of AI in Arbitration, 2025), known as the CIArb AI Guidelines, which we will analyse in more detail below. Although this advance is positive in many respects, it brings with it risks that deserve attention, namely the possibility of manipulating information and spreading disinformation. These phenomena are aggravated by the dynamic socio-political context of the leading powers in this area—the United States of America and the People's Republic of China—which could have worrying consequences for the European Union in the medium term. The EU faces two challenges: it is significantly behind the two powers mentioned in the development of AI, and it is struggling with legal and structural weaknesses. Of particular note is the near absence of a solid framework for Intellectual Property, in contrast to the predominance of Industrial Property, a remarkable paradox in a union that lacks a robust industrial base. This contradiction, which is little publicised, creates a hostile environment for innovation and technological and financial adaptation, undermining Europe's ability to compete in a global scenario marked by accelerated transformations. The discrepancy between legal priorities and current economic needs is thus proving to be a critical, albeit little publicly recognised, obstacle to the EU's progress in a context of technological revolution.

The technology associated with AI is now an unavoidable reality in all spheres of modern life, although this study focuses specifically on its application to international law and arbitration. A paradigmatic example of this transformation is the widespread use of videoconferencing in Portuguese courts, instituted by Law no. 1-A/2020 of 19 March, which allows parties, witnesses and experts to participate remotely via platforms such as Zoom, Teams or Cisco Webex Meetings. This innovation has facilitated the production of testimonial evidence and contributed to procedural efficiency, even in situations where physical presence is impossible, thus reinforcing the mechanisms for the administration of justice. Another relevant case is the HarveyAI platform, developed specifically for law firms, which exemplifies the transformative potential of AI in the legal sector.

The technologies underlying AI—such as memory algorithms, machine learning and natural language processing—are generating a paradigm shift in the practice of law. This transformation encompasses both the theoretical dimension (doctrinal research, jurisprudential analysis and academic production) and forensic practice. In the legal profession, it materialises from the initial advice to the client to the subsumption of the specific case to the legal norm, through to the drafting of pleadings, representation in court or arbitration, and strategic management of litigation until final judicial or arbitral decisions are obtained, as documented by Tai (2020). Comparable perspectives can be found in recent scholarship on AI and legal practice (Chan et al 2023; Chan and Lejiniece 2024; El Amari et al 2024; Gómez-Moreno 2024; Mühlhoff 2023; Ramírez 2024; Tu et al 2024; Van Ettekoven and Prins 2024).

AI is proving to be increasingly decisive in the handling of judicial and extra-judicial proceedings, particularly in document management, although it is not limited to this aspect. Its ability to organise and analyse large volumes of data faster than humans makes it an indispensable resource for legal professionals, complementing—and sometimes surpassing—the operational capabilities of traditional employees. In addition to procedural efficiency, AI shows potential in identifying patterns in consolidated case law, in strengthening arguments during hearings and even in creating predictive models of litigation outcomes, as studied by Pietronudo et al. (2022). However, this technological incorporation requires methodological rigour in order to preserve fundamental values such as transparency, accountability and reliability in algorithmic knowledge acquisition processes, as Huang and colleagues Huang et al. (2022) warn. Practical dilemmas thus arise: from optimising the implementation of systems to defining responsibilities for monitoring them, to the challenge of ensuring the parties' trust in the neutrality of computational processes.

This complexity requires arbitrators and jurists to make judicious use of AI, in line with the structuring principles of law and alternative dispute resolution mechanisms in a global context, as advocated by Shaw (2019). The adoption of tools such as the ethical guidelines of the Chartered Institute of Arbitrators (CIArb AI Guidelines, 2025) is an important but insufficient step in the face of the speed of digital transformation. The balance between technological innovation and preserving procedural guarantees remains the sector's great challenge, requiring adaptive regulatory frameworks that keep pace with the evolution of artificial intelligence systems without jeopardising the pillars of legal fairness.

Interestingly, on the day this book was finished—21 January 2025—US President Donald Trump publicly announced an investment of 500 billion dollars in artificial intelligence according to Reuters (21 Jan 2025), AP, and official press release through a joint venture between OpenAI, Oracle and SoftBank. The new entity, called Stargate, will start building data centres and energy infrastructures in Texas, with initial funding of 100 billion dollars, which could reach five times that amount. This project, which is going ahead despite the public disagreement between Elon Musk and the leadership of OpenAI, illustrates the geopolitical acceleration in the technology race. This initiative reinforces a broader reflection: global strategic decisions are shaped by individuals whose personal trajectories—laden with past experiences and ideological constructs—directly influence the exercise of power. When these individuals rise to positions of command, they project particular visions that condition civilisational development, and it is up to future generations to manage the consequences of these choices.

This phenomenon is replicated in the current international configuration: while the US and the Russian Federation position themselves as the architects of a New Socio-

Economic Era, the People's Republic of China and, above all, the European Union adopt a more discreet role. These geopolitical alliances and fragmentations, marked by unpredictability, redefine power dynamics in a world where macroeconomics and institutional instability are intertwined. The Stargate case thus symbolises the paradox of the digital age: exponential technological advances coexist with the permanence of human constraints—individual and collective—that continue to dictate the pace and direction of global progress.

Having made the philosophical-structural repair, I have the task of continuing the work that has now been finalised in the form of a book proper. I am fully aware that a work of this nature will quickly become outdated, given the dizzying speed of technological development—especially in hybrid quantum computing applied to AI, such as hybrid quantum processors, which give rise to so-called quantum AI, and in biological computing, responsible for the emergence of synthetic biological intelligence, the basis for a new generation of biological AI.

In the field of quantum computing, the current supremacy of the People's Republic of China stands out, which has developed a quantum chip 10^{15} times faster (a quadrillion times) than the most powerful supercomputers, equalling Google's Willow QPU. At the same time, biological computing is advancing with the first computers using human brain cells grown in the laboratory, integrated into silicon chips for complex calculations. These advances pave the way for a new paradigm in biological AI.

It's amazing how quickly quantum and biological computing are evolving. It is likely that soon after the publication of this book, new developments and updates will emerge in the field of AI on a global scale—a trend that will undoubtedly continue to accelerate. However, the central question remains: are we, the law and international arbitration, keeping up with this dynamic with the same agility and incorporating it effectively into legal and arbitration practice?

In structural terms, the book is now organised into five chapters. Following this General Introduction—Artificial Intelligence (AI) and International Arbitration, Chap. 2 addresses the multifaceted relationship between Artificial Intelligence (AI) and International Arbitration, covering topics such as videoconferencing, evidence management, machine learning, and blockchain integration. Chap. 3 shifts focus to Artificial Intelligence in Law, examining its impact on legal systems and judicial decision-making. Chap. 4 explores the role of AI in Alternative Dispute Resolution (ADR), the legal profession, and arbitration processes, with particular attention to communication, regulatory frameworks, and online dispute resolution (ODR). Chap. 5 provides a forward-looking analysis of the legal and ethical implications of AI, offering a critical perspective on the future of law and justice in the digital age. Comparable concerns are addressed in recent scholarship (Chan et al 2023; Mühlhoff 2023; Ramírez 2024; Tu et al 2024; Van Ettekoven and Prins 2024).

It is an extensive but detailed work that addresses the current problems and challenges imposed by the virtual world on the practice of law and arbitration.

The first chapter, entitled General Introduction—Artificial Intelligence (AI) and International Arbitration, explores the foundational intersection between technology and arbitration. It covers sub-themes such as the evolution of technology in international arbitration; the use of videoconferencing and the principle of immediacy; the advantages and challenges of integrating AI in legal contexts; AI's contribution to procedural efficiency; automation in evidence production; the application of machine learning in hearings; the balance between human judgment and algorithmic tools; ethical considerations; and the emergence of blockchain as a mechanism for contract formalisation.

The second chapter, Artificial Intelligence (AI) and International Arbitration, deepens the discussion by examining AI tools and platforms currently used in arbitration, analysing their impact on procedural autonomy, due process, evidentiary standards, and decision-making. It also reflects on best practices, risks, and regulatory models emerging globally to guide AI deployment in arbitration settings.

The third chapter, Artificial Intelligence in Law, explores the integration of AI into judicial systems and legal reasoning. It assesses how algorithmic tools influence judicial predictability, procedural economy, and the epistemological transformation of legal practice. It includes analysis of technological systems involved in case law management, predictive analytics, and digital reasoning, while discussing ethical, constitutional, and privacy-related implications.

The fourth chapter, The Role of AI in Alternative Dispute Resolution (ADR), the Practice of Law and International Arbitration, addresses the impact of digital technologies on legal communication, professional roles, and access to justice. It delves into mediation, conciliation, arbitration, ODR, and regulatory benchmarks such as UNCITRAL and the CIArb guidelines, while evaluating the emergence of substitute and disruptive technologies.

The fifth chapter offers a forward-looking perspective on the challenges and opportunities presented by AI in law and arbitration. It outlines normative, ethical and procedural frameworks necessary for ensuring that AI deployment aligns with the principles of fairness, transparency, and legal certainty. For recent studies on the cognitive and ethical impact of AI on judicial reasoning, see Chan et al. (2024); Tu et al. (2024); Van Ettekoven & Prins (2024); Mühlhoff (2023); Ramírez (2024). This chapter consolidates insights and presents pathways for future research and practical implementation.

Considering the scope and complexity of the topics analysed in this book, it is understood that the central objective—to demonstrate how AI can optimise the practice of law and international arbitration, as an Alternative Dispute Resolution (ADR) mechanism, promoting a reduction in time and costs and increasing accessibility, efficiency, effectiveness and procedural speed—has been achieved.

The application of machine learning algorithms, a subfield of AI that technologically reproduces the complexity of human reasoning, combined with natural language processing techniques, enables the automated analysis of large volumes of legal texts, extracting relevant data, identifying patterns and even projecting possible outcomes of cases based on precedents. AI-based systems can thus assist in legal strategy, increasing the accuracy of decisions. In addition, AI-equipped chatbots offer immediate support to users, simplifying technical steps in procedures such as international arbitration.

However, it is essential to address ethical and operational challenges. Issues such as data privacy, confidentiality in sensitive processes and transparency in algorithmic decision-making require rigorous attention, preventing the use of AI from jeopardising basic principles of law, such as fairness and procedural integrity. Regulation, such as the UNCITRAL Model Law and the guidelines of the Chartered Institute of Arbitrators (2025), has emerged as a pillar for harmonising innovation and legal certainty. The European experience in online dispute resolution (ODR) illustrates both progress and lessons on ethical and technical limits.

In short, AI redefines tools and methodologies, but its adoption requires a balance between technological potential and safeguarding essential human values. The book shows that, when integrated with discretion, artificial intelligence not only speeds up procedures, but also democratises access to justice, provided it is aligned with a robust ethical and legal framework.

References

Chan E, Bel MG, Malek B (2024) SVAMC draft guidelines on using AI in arbitration: a focus on the selection of arbitrators and arbitrators' use of AI. NY Dispute Resol Lawyer 12

Chan E, Gore KN, Jiang E (2023) Harnessing artificial intelligence in international arbitration practice. Contemp Asia Arbitr J 16:263

Chan E, Lejniece A (2024) The technological competence of arbitrators: Comp Int Legal Stud

El Amari M, Khalaf OI, Hamam H (2024) AI-Driven solutions in healthcare, education, and legal systems. EasyChair, No. 12530

Gómez-Moreno JP (2024) Advocacy for online proceedings: features of the digital world and their role in how communication is shaped in remote international arbitration. Int J Semiot Law 37(3):865–885

Huang C, Zhang Z, Mao B, Yao X (2022) An overview of artificial intelligence ethics. IEEE Trans Artif Intell 4(4):799–819

Mühlhoff R (2023) Predictive privacy: collective data protection in the context of artificial intelligence and big data. Big Data and Soc 10(1):20539517231166886

Pietronudo MC, Croidieu G, Schiavone F (2022) A solution looking for problems? A systematic literature review of the rationalizing influence of artificial intelligence on decision-making in innovation management. Technol Forecast Soc Change 182:121828

Ramírez JGC (2024) Natural language processing advancements: breaking barriers in human-computer interaction. J Artif Intell Gen Sci (JAIGS) 3(1):31–39

Shaw J (2019) Artificial intelligence and ethics. Harv Mag 30:1–11

Tai MCT (2020) The impact of artificial intelligence on human society and bioethics. Tzu Chi Med J 32(4):339–343

Tu SS, Cyphert A, Perl S (2024) Artificial Intelligence: legal reasoning, legal research and legal writing. Minn J Law Science & Technology, Forthcoming

Van Ettekoven BJ, Prins C (2024) Artificial intelligence and the judiciary system. In research handbook in data science and law. Edward Elgar Publishin pp 361–387

Chapter 2
Artificial Intelligence (AI) and International Arbitration

2.1 AI and the Evolution of Technology in International Arbitration—Videoconferencing and the Principle of Immediacy

AI, although consolidated as a field of study in the twentieth century, has more remote conceptual roots. The term artificial intelligence was formally coined in 1956 by John McCarthy, Marvin Minsky, Allen Newell and Herbert A. Simon during the historic conference at Dartmouth University, a founding milestone for the discipline. However, the theoretical foundations of AI go back to earlier contributions, such as those of British mathematician Alan Turing, a pioneer whose legacy includes the Turing Test (1950), a method proposed to assess whether a machine can exhibit intelligent behaviour indistinguishable from that of a human. In addition to his theoretical work, Turing played a crucial role in the Second World War by leading the team that deciphered the codes of the Enigma machine, a breakthrough that not only influenced computing, but also anticipated the relationship between technology and the solution of complex problems. His ideas, discussed in works such as The Turing Test (Moor 2003), remain benchmarks for ethical and technical debates in contemporary AI. Since then, AI has evolved significantly, with advances in learning algorithms, the development of neural networks and natural language processing, among others. AI is present in a number of current technologies, such as virtual assistants, recommendation systems, autonomous vehicles and aircraft, among others. The aim of AI is to develop systems and technologies that can perform tasks that normally require human intelligence, including skills such as pattern recognition, generative learning (Franceschelli and Musolesi 2024), reasoning, problem-solving, natural language understanding and decision-making. The ultimate goal of AI could be the creation of systems and machines capable of imitating human intelligence and

F. Messias, *The Practice of Law and International Arbitration in the Age of Artificial Intelligence*, SpringerBriefs in Law,
https://doi.org/10.1007/978-3-032-09127-7_2

performing tasks autonomously, bringing benefits to society in general and to areas such as health, finance, education, industrial and manufacturing sectors, among others.

AI has been a fast-growing field in recent years, with applications in various sectors. However, the legal implications and challenges associated with this technology have attracted significant attention. Understanding the main legal aspects of AI is key to ensuring its proper use.

One of the relevant legal issues related to AI is civil liability. Unlike conventional software, autonomous AI systems can make decisions and act independently, which raises questions about who should be held liable in the event of damage or errors caused by these technologies. For example, if an autonomous vehicle causes an accident, would it be possible to blame the manufacturer or the system itself? This dilemma highlights the complexity of legal issues involving AI (Pagallo 2018).

The legal definition of liability in the field of AI becomes complex when autonomous systems act in ways not easily attributable to human agents. Establishing a clear legal basis for AI liability is essential to ensure that the benefits of the technology are enjoyed in a balanced way, while guaranteeing the protection of individuals from possible harm (Soyer and Tettenborn 2022). On the other hand, issues such as data protection and privacy emerge as critical challenges in this area (Yanamala et al. 2024).

AI systems often require large volumes of personal data to generate predictions or make informed decisions. This raises questions about the collection, storage and processing of this data, requiring strict compliance with data protection legislation (Mühlhoff 2023). In this sense, it is crucial to analyse how these systems manage sensitive data, ensuring not only that adequate and informed consent is obtained, but also that the rights of data subjects are fully respected. At the same time, regulatory frameworks must keep pace with the rapid pace of technological advances, with a view to ensuring the protection of privacy and promoting the ethical use of information (Kingston 2017).

In addition, AI represents a challenge for legislation in the area of Intellectual Property (IP) (Lee et al. 2021). Works generated by AI systems, such as paintings, novels or music, raise issues related to Copyright and Related Rights (Mikalonytė and Kneer 2022). The complexity lies in determining whether AI should be recognised as a legitimate creator, requiring an in-depth analysis of the IP legal framework, especially Copyright. An emblematic example is the current Spotify controversy over the distribution of royalties, driven by the proliferation of AI-produced music and the emergence of virtual artists created by algorithms.

Additionally, the use of AI to automate tasks—such as patent searches—raises debates about the patentability of inventions developed by autonomous systems (Schuster, 2018). The absence of a human agent in the conception of these inventions challenges the traditional principles of IP law, which has historically attributed authorship to physical or legal entities.

Faced with these challenges, legal analysis becomes essential to define the limits of Intellectual Property protection and respond to the emerging risks posed by AI.

Jurists and legal professionals need to master the legal aspects of this technology in order to operate in a scenario of constant technological evolution. Topics such as civil liability, data privacy and copyright ownership stand out as priority issues in the legal debate on AI.

In this context, there is an urgent need to create a regulatory framework that balances stimulating technological innovation with safeguarding fundamental rights and constitutional guarantees. An effective approach to these challenges will allow society to harness the potential of AI without compromising ethical or legal values (Mariani and Dwivedi 2024).

The development of technology in International Arbitration has undergone significant changes, improving the efficiency of alternative dispute and conflict resolution processes. Faced with increasing globalisation and the complexity of commercial transactions, it has become essential to adapt technological advances to the demands of the modern world. One of the most significant advances is the emergence of online alternative dispute resolution platforms, which have revolutionised the conduct of arbitrations (Androulaki 2023).

These platforms offer parties the convenience and flexibility to participate in arbitrations remotely, reducing travel costs and saving time. In addition, the introduction of AI tools has made big data analysis, legal research and the drafting of legal documents more accurate and efficient.

One of the most significant technological advances in International Arbitration is the use of videoconferencing and teleconferencing (Gómez-Moreno 2024). These means have made it possible to overcome geographical barriers between the parties, arbitrators and experts, making the resolution of cross-border disputes more accessible and economical. Videoconferencing, for example, reproduces personal interaction in real time, simulating physical presence during hearings, which reinforces collaboration and communication in proceedings.

The incorporation of electronic systems for presenting evidence has also brought significant improvements, facilitating the display of complex documents, technical demonstrations and multimedia resources. This advance has contributed to a more agile and visually intuitive arbitration process (Alessa 2022).

At the same time, the digitisation of case management systems (Loebbecke 2021) and the implementation of virtual courtrooms have established themselves as essential pillars for technological progress in this field. These innovations not only optimise the organisation of cases, but also ensure greater transparency and efficiency, adapting to the demands of the international context (Wienrich et al. 2022).

Case management systems allow for the efficient organisation and storage of documents, simplifying case administration and ensuring easy access to information for all parties involved. Virtual courtrooms recreate the atmosphere of face-to-face hearings, providing secure and intuitive interfaces so that parties can fulfil their procedural obligations remotely. In addition, these rooms are equipped with real-time transcription and translation services, reinforcing transparency and accessibility in the arbitration process (Jain 2022).

To summarise, technological advances in International Arbitration have brought about a profound transformation in alternative dispute resolution at a global level. The implementation of digital platforms for conflict mediation, teleconferencing, digitalised management systems and virtual courtrooms has contributed to greater efficiency, cost reduction and democratisation of access to justice (Rajendra and Thuraisingam 2022). Therefore, in the face of continuous technological evolution, it is essential that professionals keep up to date and take advantage of these tools to respond to the growing demand for international arbitration.

This issue is directly related to the principle of immediacy. This principle is rooted in a global philosophical movement regarding the design of civil procedure, which originated in the French Revolution. In this context, principles such as publicity, the reasoning behind judicial decisions, orality and the free assessment of evidence are opposed to the idea of a secretive, written process, mediated by intermediaries and based on pre-defined evidence. In Portugal, this model was enshrined in the 1939 Code of Civil Procedure and is essentially maintained in the procedural legislation in force to this day.

In terms of its specificity, immediacy means a direct relationship between the judge and the evidence, whether personal or material. In the context of personal evidence, it implies that the court evaluates the oral testimony of witnesses, experts or parties on the spot, without recourse to written records. Thus, immediacy is closely linked to orality. In material evidence, on the other hand, an immediate relationship is established between the court and the object, document or place being analysed, as is the case with judicial inspections. From a broad perspective, the principle is not limited to interaction with evidence, but also covers sources of personal evidence.

Although immediacy and orality may seem to overlap in the treatment of personal evidence, they are not entirely equivalent. Orality is, to a certain extent, broader—as it applies as the standard form of various procedural acts (such as sanitation or the condensation of proceedings in a prior hearing), in addition to the production of evidence. On the other hand, it is more restricted, as it does not encompass the material dimension of immediacy.

The principle of immediacy, in its broad sense, transcends mere orality, encompassing the court's direct relationship not only with personal evidence, but also with material evidence, as well as the link between the facts alleged and the sources of evidence used (objective sense of immediacy). To ensure its effectiveness, other principles complement this framework. Concentration, for example, avoids the temporal dispersion of pre-trial acts, determining that they should preferably take place in a single hearing (arts. 604, no. 3; 456, no. 1; and 500 of the Code of Civil Procedure, henceforth CPC). The continuity of the hearing requires that any interruptions be brief (Articles 606(2) and (3) CPC), while publicity (Article 606(1) CPC) and the full assistance of the judge (Article 605 CPC) ensure that the evidence is produced before the court that will decide the case.

Immediacy is justified by the need for the judge to have access to more reliable evidence, thus realising the principle of free assessment of the evidence (art. 607, no. 5 CPC). Based on the perceptions gathered during the production of the evidence and guided by the maxims of experience, the judge forms his conviction—a process that requires direct contact with the evidence, without mediations that distort his understanding. This conviction, although subjective, is formalised through the reasoning behind the decision, making the logical reasoning behind it transparent.

In the case of personal evidence, immediacy makes it possible to capture nuances that transcend the written record: hesitations, changes in tone of voice, body posture, facial expressions or even changes in the colour of the face (blushing, paleness). These elements, which are not transferable by documents, are decisive in forming a free and informed judgment, ensuring that the decision reflects an authentic assessment of the facts.

2.2 Integration of AI in Law and International Arbitration

In the field of law and international arbitration, technological advances have revolutionised dispute resolution, increasing the efficiency, accessibility and transparency of proceedings. One notable innovation is virtual hearings via videoconferencing platforms, which eliminate geographical barriers and allow parties in different countries to participate remotely (Alarie et al. 2018). In addition to reducing travelling costs and time, these solutions promote the inclusion of diverse participants, reinforcing the global nature of arbitration.

Another relevant milestone is the integration of AI tools into procedural management systems. These technologies process large volumes of data quickly, analyse precedents and offer predictive insights to arbitrators, helping them make decisions. In addition, resources such as machine translation mitigate language barriers during proceedings, ensuring clear communication between the parties (Villata et al. 2022).

At the same time, blockchain technology is emerging as a pillar of security and transparency. By storing evidence immutably and tracking all procedural steps in real time, this solution ensures integrity and accountability, critical elements for the credibility of the system (Kumar et al. 2021).

Taken together, these innovations redefine International Arbitration: they speed up procedures, reduce operating costs, democratise access to justice and strengthen fairness between players. Earlier reflections on the normative evolution of AI in law and arbitration can be found in Bali (1974) and McCarthy (1955), while more recent analyses (El Amari et al 2024; Chan et al. 2024; Pant & Ahmad 2022; Soyer 2024; Tai 2020; Van Ettekoven & Prins 2024) further explore the legal-ethical dimensions of algorithmic governance. The result is a more agile, inclusive and reliable system that benefits all parties involved and consolidates arbitration as the preferred mechanism for cross-border disputes (Kop 2021; Ejjami 2024).

2.3 Advantages and Challenges of AI in Law and International Arbitration

The advent of AI in international arbitration presents significant advantages and challenges (Waqar 2022). Among the benefits is the ability to increase the efficiency and accuracy of arbitration proceedings (Srivastava 2021).

AI makes it possible to analyse large volumes of data, identify patterns and generate agile and reliable predictions, thus optimising decision-making by arbitrators (Kasap 2021). In addition, it speeds up document review, facilitates the identification of relevant evidence and reduces manual workload (Ashley 2017), as well as assisting in the drafting of pleadings (Hricik et al. 2017).

However, the implementation of AI in this field is not without its obstacles. The main concern lies in ensuring transparency and accountability, especially when complex algorithms operate without direct human supervision (Alsamara and Ghazi 2024). There are also legitimate concerns about privacy and security, given the handling of confidential information. Finding a balance between the benefits of AI and the inherent risks is an additional challenge for industry professionals.

A balanced approach, combining specialised knowledge and machine learning, could mitigate these challenges, promoting a harmonious integration between technology and arbitration practice (Davida and Lubasz 2021).

2.4 The Role of AI in International Arbitration and Efficiency in Arbitration Proceedings

The integration of AI in International Arbitration has revolutionised the efficiency and accuracy of proceedings, although it presents complex challenges. AI demonstrates the ability to analyse massive volumes of data, identify patterns and generate agile predictions, optimising decision-making (Kasap 2021). In addition to speeding up document review and evidence identification (Ashley 2017), it assists in drafting pleadings (Hricik et al. 2017), allowing lawyers to focus on strategic aspects (Colorado 2023).

However, the reliance on unsupervised algorithms raises critical questions about transparency and accountability (Alsamara and Ghazi 2024). Additionally, the handling of sensitive data requires stringent privacy and security safeguards. A balance between machine learning and human expertise emerges as a promising solution to mitigate risks (Davida and Lubasz 2021).

AI also redefines legal predictability: algorithms analyse case law and historical cases, offering predictive insights that guide litigation or settlement strategies (Onyefulu 2023). This thorough analysis reduces cognitive bias, ensuring decisions based on objective standards (Gulyamov and Bakhramova 2022). The traceability of the decision-making process—through immutable records—enhances transparency, allowing parties to understand the logic behind decisions.

Although AI should not replace human judgment, its potential to streamline procedures, reduce costs and increase fairness is undeniable (Florescu 2024). Technology promises a future where arbitration is not only faster, but also more accessible and reliable, consolidating itself as the preferred mechanism for cross-border disputes (Solhchi and Baghbanno 2023).

2.5 Automation of Administrative Tasks and Management in the Production of Evidence by AI

AI-based tools are revolutionising arbitral and judicial proceedings by fully automating administrative routines, from procedural management to party notification, optimising human and technical resources (Lee 2022). Specialised doctrine underlines the proven effectiveness of these systems in streamlining workflows, allowing legal operators to devote themselves to substantive issues of greater technical complexity, according to recent studies by Nikolskaia and Naumov (2020).

The application of machine learning algorithms makes it possible to predictively analyse legal macro-data, with natural language processing capabilities that allow for the automated extraction of relevant information from contracts, epistolary communication and financial documentation. This technology proves particularly useful in evidence management, where it identifies patterns and anomalies in large volumes of data, as demonstrated by Chan et al. (2023) in their analysis of AI-assisted e-discovery.

Intelligent systems also incorporate integrated procedural management functionalities, including automatic scheduling of court acts, control of court deadlines and assisted generation of procedural acts, ensuring strict compliance with the requirements of the Code of Civil Procedure. Implementing these solutions exponentially reduces the risk of nullity due to formal defects, while at the same time guaranteeing efficiency gains that can be quantified in institutional productivity metrics.

In addition, AI platforms offer analytical tools for monitoring institutional performance, allowing courts to identify procedural bottlenecks and implement systemic improvements based on empirical evidence. This strategic dimension reinforces the transparency of the administration of justice, in line with the requirements of the Statute on the Organisation and Functioning of the Judicial Courts.

In the sphere of interaction with users, virtual assistants capable of providing basic legal information on a continuous basis, ensuring standardised responses to frequent queries about deadlines, costs or procedural requirements, stand out. This feature, analysed by Alkhayer et al. (2023), makes the principle of efficiency enshrined in Article 8 of the Law on the Organisation of the Judicial System a reality. Technological evolution also introduces predictive mechanisms for assessing legal risk, cross-referencing consolidated case law with specific case parameters to generate statistically based prognoses. This tool aids strategic decision-making, without prejudice to the indispensable human judgment.

To summarise, the responsible integration of AI systems into legal-administrative workflows is a transformative paradigm, boosting speed gains, reducing unnecessary litigation and strengthening legal certainty, always in strict compliance with the constitutional principles of due process set out in Article 20 of the Constitution of the Portuguese Republic.

2.6 The Use of AI in the Practice of Law

AI is revolutionising the field of legal research and case analysis, significantly increasing lawyers' efficiency and accuracy. AI-powered platforms have the remarkable ability to process large volumes of legal documents in a fraction of the time it would take a human, saving valuable hours of painstaking research. These platforms use advanced machine learning algorithms to identify patterns and extract data from legal documents, allowing lawyers to quickly locate relevant precedents, statutes and case law (Araluce 2024).

In addition, AI-based tools enhance case analysis by revealing connections between cases that might otherwise go unnoticed by human researchers. By identifying these hidden relationships, AI enables lawyers to strengthen their arguments and develop more convincing strategies for their clients. The incorporation of technology in this field also guarantees consistency in legal research, eliminating human errors and biases that could jeopardise the results. In this way, by integrating AI into their routines, professionals can produce high-quality work with maximum efficiency (Lindes 2020).

It is worth highlighting the differences between Level 1 and Level 2 AI. Level 1 AI, often referred to as 'basic AI' or 'narrow AI', refers to systems designed for specific tasks, with limited capabilities compared to more advanced levels. Examples include chatbots, recommendation systems and simple image recognition software. These systems operate on the basis of predefined rules or machine learning algorithms, with no capacity for continuous learning beyond their initial programming. They therefore require human supervision to deal with situations outside their scope (Deroy et al. 2024).

Level 2 AI, or 'advanced AI', represents a more sophisticated level. Its systems use neural networks, deep learning and natural language processing to understand and generate complex texts. Unlike Level 1, they adapt to new situations without human intervention and achieve comparable or superior performance to humans in specific tasks—as demonstrated by DeepMind's AlphaGo, which mastered the complex strategy game Go (Mustapha 2024).

In practice, AI applied to law makes it possible to analyse large volumes of legal data in reduced time, helping lawyers to identify critical information quickly. As well as saving time, the tools update professionals in real time on legal changes, guaranteeing precise guidance in line with client requirements. In this way, technology not only optimises processes, but also expands technical expertise, raising the quality of legal services.

2.7 Understanding the Concept of Machine Learning and Its Application to the Adjudication Hearing

The incorporation of machine learning, as a branch of AI, has revolutionised jurisprudence through the use of data and algorithms to support reasoned judicial decisions. Earlier reflections on AI in jurisprudence (McCarthy 1955; Bali 1974) already anticipated the challenges later examined by Chan and Lejiniece (2024) and Soyer (2024). This technology allows judges to analyse massive volumes of information and identify patterns that would otherwise escape human analysis. By training models with extensive data sets, machine learning algorithms assimilate knowledge from previous cases, making predictions about future outcomes with a high degree of accuracy. In the context of adjudication, the applications are multifaceted: from predicting sentences based on the seriousness of the offence and the profile of the defendant to assessing the reliability of testimonies. Automating these functions reduces the risk of human bias, increases procedural efficiency and guarantees greater uniformity in decisions.

The combination of algorithmic capacity and the human perspective aims to achieve a fairer and more equitable judicial system. Algorithms help judges make predictions based on empirical data and detect patterns that are not immediately recognisable. However, the effectiveness of these tools is intrinsically linked to the quality of the training data and can perpetuate existing distortions in the information bases. For this reason, judges must critically scrutinise the results generated, ensuring that they comply with legal principles and material fairness. In addition, the human element introduces dimensions that are irreducible to algorithmic coding, such as empathetic capacity, discretion in weighing up mitigating circumstances and adapting to complex contexts that go beyond the binary logic of machines.

2.8 The Balance Between Technological Innovation and Judicial Discernment Is Therefore Imperative for Preserving the Integrity of the Legal System

In the field of International Arbitration, predictive analysis is emerging as a transformative decision-making tool. By processing historical data, machine learning algorithms identify trends and correlations that subsidise arbitrators in their decision-making. These predictive models make it possible, for example, to assess the legal viability of arguments, anticipate the optimum time for settlement negotiations or recommend the selection of arbitrators based on previously mapped decision-making profiles. The impact of this technology can be seen in the increase in procedural efficiency, the reduction of informational asymmetries and the promotion of transparency, factors that converge to optimise results. Despite the inherent challenges—such as personal data protection issues and the need for statistical validation of sources—the benefits associated with predictive analysis are unavoidable. As technology evolves and the legal community recognises its operational value, this tool will become an indispensable element in reconfiguring the future landscape of international arbitration, always subject to respect for the principles of independence, impartiality and due process of law.

2.9 Ethics and Morality in the Use of AI

The integration of AI systems in arbitration raises fundamental ethical questions that require a careful balance between technological efficiency and indispensable human intervention. Although AI has demonstrated remarkable capabilities in analysing large volumes of data, predicting scenarios and streamlining decision-making processes, its application in this field faces structural limitations that can only be mitigated through active human participation.

The complex nature of arbitration—which involves interpreting legal norms, assessing behaviour and intentions, and weighing up specific cultural contexts—requires a discernment that algorithms cannot fully replicate. AI systems, despite their quantitative rigour, are subject to intrinsic biases arising from the historical data used to train them, which can perpetuate systemic inequalities. In addition, the opacity of many algorithms (black boxes) jeopardises the transparency required in arbitration processes, creating challenges for ethical and legal accountability (Browning and John 2024).

Human intervention is crucial in three main dimensions. Firstly, in the critical detection of algorithmic errors or biases that could distort the results. Secondly, in incorporating subjective factors—such as the credibility of witnesses or cultural nuances—that escape purely statistical analysis. Finally, ensuring that decisions respect standards of fairness and empathy, values that machines do not internalise on their own. This synergy makes it possible, for example, for multi-party international arbitrations to adequately consider linguistic and normative differences, ensuring that cultural diversity is reflected in the final decisions (Kapoor et al. 2024).

Ethical concerns also extend to the sphere of privacy and data security. The processing of sensitive information by AI systems requires robust protocols to prevent unauthorised access or misuse, in compliance with regulations such as the General Data Protection Regulation (GDPR). At the same time, there is a need to clarify accountability mechanisms: as the systems gain autonomy, it becomes urgent to define who is responsible for any failures—be it the system developers, the operators or the arbitration institutions themselves (Tu et al. 2024).

The solution lies in a hybrid model that combines the analytical capacity of AI with continuous human supervision. Such an approach requires periodic audits of algorithms to identify emerging biases, the implementation of explainable systems (XAI) that make technological decisions comprehensible to the parties involved, and the formation of multidisciplinary committees capable of assessing wider social impacts. Only through this complementarity will it be possible to preserve public trust, ensuring that AI-assisted arbitration does not sacrifice substantive justice for the sake of mere procedural efficiency (Artikova 2024).

Ultimately, the human comparative advantage lies in the ability to contextualise abstract legal principles, adapt decisions to exceptional circumstances and safeguard the dignity of the parties—dimensions that, however advanced the technology, remain in the irrevocable domain of ethical judgment.

2.10 The Role of AI and Human Judgment in the Arbitration Process

The integration of AI into international arbitration presents a modern paradox: while it promises to revolutionise procedural efficiency through automated data analysis and pattern prediction, it requires uncompromising human safeguarding to preserve substantive fairness. The crux of this discussion lies in the recognition that algorithms, despite their statistical rigour, lack the holistic ability to interpret cultural contexts, linguistic nuances and subjective intentions—crucial elements in disputes involving multiple jurisdictions.

Human experience remains irreplaceable in detecting hidden algorithmic biases, a particularly worrying phenomenon when systems are trained with historical data that mirrors structural discriminations. As Browning and John (2024) point out, the uncritical replication of these patterns through tools such as Arbitrus—a pioneering platform in automated arbitration—can crystallise injustices if not mediated by continuous human audits. This need becomes pressing in complex scenarios such as criminal mega-proceedings, where AI helps sort through thousands of documents, but requires supervision to avoid decontextualising evidence.

The emergence of legal prompt engineering—a technique that adapts textual instructions to optimise interaction with generative systems such as DALL-E—illustrates both the potential and the risks of this technological symbiosis. While digital discovery tools speed up the evidentiary production phase, as provided for in the IBA Rules on the Taking of Evidence, the final interpretation of multilingual contracts or the weighing up of conflicting testimonies remain essentially human domains. Kapoor et al. (2024) warn that the efficiency gained in analysing documents must not compromise the fundamental right to understand the motivations behind decisions, calling for explainable systems (XAI) that make algorithmic logic transparent.

The ethical implications extend to the sphere of privacy: the processing of sensitive data by platforms such as Arbitrus requires GDPR-compliant protocols, particularly in cross-border arbitrations where different legal regimes collide. Tu et al. (2024) emphasise that cyber security must be a priority, given the risk of data breaches that could compromise strategic business secrets. At the same time, there is a debate about civil liability—when a predictive system recommends a disadvantageous agreement based on biased data, will the blame fall on developers, operators or arbitration institutions?

The solution lies in a hybrid model where AI acts as a cognitive assistant, never as an autonomous decision-making entity. In practice, this means first and foremost: using algorithms for initial screening of evidence and identification of relevant case law, reserving to human arbitrators the assessment of testimonial credibility and intercultural fairness, and implementing multidisciplinary ethical committees to monitor decision-making standards.

The Portuguese experience in the Courts of Peace demonstrates how digital tools can speed up processes without eliminating human mediation—a valuable lesson for international contexts. However, as Artikova (2024) warns, this transition requires massive investment in the technical training of jurists, enabling them both to challenge algorithmic conclusions and to exploit the analytical potential of systems such as IBM Watson in detecting contractual inconsistencies.

The near future will require redefining essential skills: while once a good arbitrator mastered oratory and legal exegesis, today they must understand the basics of data science without losing the ability to empathise strategically. This duality is reflected in the growing demand for technological compliance specialists, capable of translating ethical requirements into programme parameters.

Ultimately, the real challenge is not to replace human judgment with machines, but to prevent the lure of technological efficiency from obscuring the primary purpose of arbitration: to resolve disputes with contextualised justice, preserving international commercial relations in an increasingly fragmented world. As Sharma (2024) summarises, AI in arbitration should be compared not to a robotic judge, but to a digital telescope—it amplifies human vision, but does not replace the discernment of those who wield it.

2.11 The Impact of AI on Legal Professionals

The integration of AI systems into international arbitration poses ethical and operational challenges that require a delicate balance between technological innovation and preserving the humanistic values of law. Although AI demonstrates exceptional capabilities in the predictive analysis of data and the automation of procedural tasks—such as the sorting of documents in mega cases or the identification of patterns in case law—its practical application comes up against structural limitations. Algorithms, trained on historical data that often reflects systemic biases, lack the innate ability to interpret cultural nuances or contextualise human intentions, as Browning and John (2024) point out. This gap makes human oversight indispensable, particularly in multi-party arbitrations where language collisions and normative differences require intercultural and multicultural sensitivity.

In the broader field of legal practice, AI redefines professional competences without replacing the essential core of legal activity. Tools such as Thomson-Reuters' CoCounsel or Lexis + AI have revolutionised legal research by reducing hours of manual due diligence work. However, as Liu (2024) notes, the interpretation of rules in the light of constitutional principles or strategic negotiation remain areas where human empathy is irreplaceable. The Portuguese experience in the Courts of Peace demonstrates how digital platforms can speed up processes without eliminating face-to-face mediation—a valuable lesson for complex international contexts.

The future will require jurists to have a dual competence: technical mastery to interrogate algorithmic systems and human sagacity to challenge biased conclusions. This duality is reflected in the growing demand for specialists in technological compliance, capable of translating ethical demands into programme parameters. As Sharma (2024) summarises, AI in arbitration is akin to a digital telescope—it expands analytical vision, but does not replace the discernment of those who wield it.

Ultimately, the challenge goes beyond mere procedural optimisation. It is a question of ensuring that the digital revolution in arbitration does not sacrifice substantive fairness on the altar of efficiency, preserving the role of the human being as the ultimate guardian of contextualised justice. Technology, when calibrated with ethical wisdom, can not only speed up procedures, but also deepen access to justice on a global scale—as long as it is kept under the irrevocable scrutiny of human judgment.

In addition, the use of AI in the legal field can generate cost savings for law firms and clients. The automation of routine tasks allows these firms to reduce their dependence on large teams, resulting in lower operating costs. This efficiency, in turn, tends to make legal services more accessible and affordable, especially for clients who were previously put off by high fees.

However, it is crucial to emphasise that while AI can significantly enhance legal practice, it should not replace human lawyers entirely. The professional experience, capacity for contextualised judgment and empathy inherent in human beings remain irreplaceable. Thus, AI should be understood as a complementary tool—capable of supporting and optimising lawyers' work—and not as a substitute for their technical knowledge and insight (Cyran 2024; Posthoff 2024).

2.12 Prompts and Language Models: A Tool for Drafting, Reviewing and Interpreting Contracts

The rise of Large Language Models (LLMs) in the field of generative artificial intelligence and the practice of creating prompts to generate ideal responses from these models are transforming legal practice. The use of LLMs to draft contractual clauses, interpret ambiguous terms in contracts and review legal documents raises new questions about the interaction between these prompts and the parol evidence rule. This rule, a principle of common law jurisdictions, restricts the types of evidence that parties can invoke in a contractual dispute to define the terms of a written agreement. Once the written contract has been finalised, the rule in principle prevents the parties from presenting extrinsic evidence—such as oral discussions, preliminary emails or negotiation drafts—to modify or contradict the terms of the document. The aim is to ensure that the written contract, when conceived as the complete and final expression of the agreement, prevails over any previous oral or informal disagreements. The central maxim of the rule—extrinsic evidence is inadmissible to alter a written contract—takes on nuances in the context of LLMs. For example: If a prompt used to generate a contractual clause reveals an intention not reflected in the final text, could this be considered extrinsic evidence? How do you balance AI-generated interpretation with the principle that the written document is definitive?

The term parol, of Anglo-Norman origin (parol/parole, verbal), historically refers to the priority of the written over the oral. Today, this debate extends to digital: to what extent can prompts, algorithms or AI metadata be equated with extrinsic evidence in the context of the rule?

Today, LLMs offer a glimpse of a future where contracts are not merely drafted, but articulated through algorithms capable of analysing complex legal contexts. For example, models such as GPT-4 can generate legal texts indistinguishable from human essays, synthesising legislation, case law and technical terms in a few seconds. This advance democratises access to the law: non-lawyers can understand legal obligations thanks to simplified explanations, while law firms use these tools to optimise contract reviews, comparing clauses with reference databases to assess risks or compliance.

However, the practical application of LLMs comes up against delicate issues. A central challenge lies in the tension between algorithmic interpretation and contractual intent. Suppose a prompt used to generate a clause reveals an intention not reflected in the final text: could this data be considered extrinsic evidence, inadmissible under the parol testimony rule? Moreover, LLMs operate by lexical probability, not legal understanding, which can lead to clauses that are superficially coherent but misaligned with critical legal nuances. Responsibility for any errors also remains unclear—would it lie with the lawyer, the model developer or the AI itself?

To mitigate these risks, prompt engineering—a technique that involves the careful drafting of instructions to guide LLMs—becomes essential. A practical example is the creation of hierarchical prompts, such as 'Prioritise confidentiality clauses according to case law X', ensuring alignment with legal standards. Combining automatic generation with human review focused on contractual intent is another crucial strategy, as is documenting the prompts used, creating a digital history that can serve as a reference in future disputes.

Functionally, LLMs are trained in two phases. In the initial phase, they are exposed to millions of texts (laws, contracts, articles) to internalise linguistic patterns. Next, lawyers adjust them with annotated examples, such as 'This non-compete clause is typical in labour contracts', refining their ability to generate legally robust content. Continuous self-learning allows the model to identify contextual relationships between terms (e.g. 'indemnity' → 'civil liability'), simulating legal reasoning to some extent.

This scenario requires a dynamic adaptation of the law. If historically the parol testimony rule prioritised the written over the oral, today the debate extends to the digital: prompts, AI metadata and even the source code of models could theoretically be invoked as extrinsic evidence to challenge a contract. As courts face cases such as 'State v. Algorithm X' (hypothetical), where an AI-generated contract is disputed on the basis of the instructions that produced it, jurisprudence will have to delimit the extent to which technology redefines—or not—the core principles of contract law.

Large Language Models (LLMs) operate through advanced word embedding processes, which group semantically close terms together to map contextual relationships between them. These associations—such as the link between contract and clause or between indemnity and civil liability—allow the model to assign specific functions to each word within a sentence, determining the overall meaning of the text. When given an input, these models predict the most likely sequence of words based on the patterns assimilated during training. However, this probabilistic approach reveals limitations in novel scenarios not covered by the training data, leading the model to prioritise frequent lexical combinations, even in contexts that require adaptation to legal novelties or legal creativity.

The underlying architecture of these systems—the transformers (origin of the 'T' in GPT)—uses deep neural networks to process language non-sequentially, analysing all the words in a text simultaneously. This capability makes it possible, for example, to identify how a pronoun in the preamble of a contract refers to a term defined in the final clauses. Training is divided into two critical phases: in a first pre-training stage, the model is exposed to a massive, generic corpus (books, articles, legal documents) to internalise basic linguistic patterns; later, in the fine-tuning phase, experts adjust it with specific data (such as software licence agreements or labour case law), refining its aptitude for tasks such as classifying intentions in clauses, generating legal questions/answers or extracting information from documents.

In the legal domain, this flexibility allows LLMs to process the technical language of law—full of Latin formulae, complex syntactic structures and specialised terms—with apparent precision. A fine-tuned model in merger and acquisition contracts can, for example, generate contextualised confidentiality clauses or detect inconsistencies between the definition of confidential information. However, the reliance on historical data introduces a hindsight bias: models trained on pre-2020 contracts may ignore recent legislative updates, such as the General Data Protection Regulation (GDPR). In addition, the emphasis on lexical probabilities can generate illusions of coherence—texts that are well structured semantically but legally unworkable. Imagine an LLM drafting an arbitration clause that is internally consistent but incompatible with the law of the chosen forum, a situation that would require human intervention to correct.

The evolution of these models raises fascinating questions about the future of contractual drafting. If, on the one hand, they make it possible to democratise access to clear legal documents for non-lawyers, on the other, they challenge traditional notions such as authorship and intent. An AI-generated contract, based on prompts drawn up by a lawyer, would raise questions about which element—the final text, the prompt's instructions or the model's algorithm—should prevail in the event of a conflict. This dilemma echoes historical debates in contract law, such as those raised by the parol testimony rule, but transposed to a digital age where the spoken word has become an algorithmic code.

In order for a large language model (LLM) to provide useful output to the user, it needs to respond to a prompt—a textual instruction that includes context, examples or specific guidelines about the desired result. Optimising these instructions, known as prompt engineering, allows the model to be adapted to different tasks. When there are few examples in the prompt, the model operates in few-trial learning; without examples, in zero-trial learning. Despite these limitations, GPT-3 has demonstrated the ability to generate coherent and humanised texts, even with minimal prompts, thanks to its training on vast volumes of data. This performance comes from parameters (internal variables adjusted during training) that have evolved exponentially: from 117 million in GPT-1 to 175 billion in GPT-3. It is currently speculated that models such as GPT-4 will exceed 100 trillion parameters, increasing their ability to process natural language in an agile and contextualised way. This advance is enhanced by training on large bodies of text and refinement via 'Reinforcement Learning with Human Feedback (RLHF)', a technique that aligns the model's responses to human expectations. Thus, even with concise instructions, modern LLMs combine computational scale and algorithmic sophistication to deliver fluid and precise interactions.

Given the adaptation to legal language, there is a specific training process to develop generic language models that are then specialised for the legal sector, enabling the generation of contractual provisions. Law firms have started training local language models, such as Vicuna, keeping them isolated from external services. This approach not only differentiates their automation processes and service offerings, but also resolves client confidentiality and data privacy issues associated with using public models. Since the rapid adoption of OpenAI's ChatGPT 3.5 from the end of 2022, language models have gained significant relevance in legal practice.

The ability of these systems to articulate contractual obligations requires them to replicate two essential strands of legal work. Firstly, they need to translate instructions into legal texts, generating contractual provisions from their training data set, which automates the drafting of clauses that reflect the agreements negotiated between the parties. Secondly, they must interpret multiple contractual provisions to ensure compliance, iteratively analysing user inputs and adjusting outputs in subsequent prompts. This process ensures that the end result is fit for purpose and aligned with the negotiation objectives.

In addition to drafting, language models show potential for interpreting ambiguous contractual terms in a more agile way than traditional methods, which often fail to keep up with the dynamic evolution of contract management or legal interpretations. They therefore represent a promising tool for modernising legal practices, balancing technical efficiency with the ethical and professional demands of the law.

The emerging nexus between large-scale language models (LLMs) and contract law offers a glimpse of a future in which contracts are drafted by algorithms, with precision enhanced by prompt engineering. One of the most significant advantages of AI-assisted drafting lies in its unrivalled speed and efficiency, particularly visible in complex contexts such as drafting contracts for large infrastructure projects, known for their length and intricate technicality. LLMs, trained in vast legal corpora, can identify model clauses suited to a client's specific risk profile, detect terminological inconsistencies, cross-reference scheduled subcontracts and suggest alternative wordings at a pace that surpasses even the most experienced professional. These capabilities amplify the pressure on lawyers to adopt these tools, given their potential to increase the value of transactions by reducing procedural inefficiencies.

It is important, however, to distinguish AI-assisted drafting from smart contracts, the latter being self-executing blockchain-based agreements programmed to automate obligations when pre-defined conditions are met—such as automatic payments upon delivery of goods or smart storage mechanisms. Although there are efforts to converge AI and blockchain, a clear demarcation persists: smart contracts function as deterministic algorithms integrated into distributed ledger ecosystems, including Decentralised Autonomous Organisations (DAOs), which coordinate commercial activities through algorithmic execution, while LLMs focus on textual genesis and refinement.

Within the scope of revising contractual clauses, two main techniques stand out. The first involves analysing the similarity between a specific clause and examples taken from reliable sources, such as a law firm's internal precedents, replicating the work of juniors who adjust models to concrete cases. The second technique takes advantage of LLMs' ability to extract key phrases from massive volumes of documents, ensuring terminological consistency and adherence to legal principles, minimising ambiguities and unintended gaps. Additionally, these models identify points that require legislative updates or contextual adjustments, even in documents with heterogeneous styles. By employing natural language processing techniques, they also detect grammatical errors or syntactical inconsistencies that might otherwise go unnoticed, increasing the rigour of textual production. This meticulousness drastically reduces the risk of typographical errors or confusing wording, resulting in more precise and polished final documents. Although word processing tools have existed in the legal market for more than a decade, LLMs introduce an additional layer of sophistication, allowing not just static analysis, but dynamic drafting suggestions that transform legal practice, balancing technical innovation with the ethical and professional demands of the field.

Generative AI offers the promise of reducing legal costs in a number of ways, in line with current trends. AI-assisted or even autonomous contract drafting—even if limited to standardised provisions—can support contract standardisation in the construction industry, combining flexibility for customised amendments tailored to the specific needs of each project. By providing pre-filled templates tailored to particular types of projects, with variables and prompts for customising clauses, LLMs ensure consistency and clarity, while maintaining the adaptability needed to align with risk profiles and liability allocations typical of the sector. This scalability proves especially valuable in large-scale projects involving multiple subcontracts, by streamlining contracting processes across the entire project ecosystem, promoting interoperability and reducing discrepancies. At the same time, automating the review of contractual clauses could enable wide-ranging adjustments to pre-existing models, ensuring that changes maintain fairness and legal compliance, paving the way for integrating smart contracts—self-executing blockchain-based agreements that automate obligations when pre-defined conditions are met. In practice, such contracts can manage phased payments in construction projects, monitor material deliveries or resolve disputes automatically, optimising management and fostering trust between parties. However, an emerging challenge lies in the growing use of generative AI by non-lawyers to interpret, reformulate and document agreements without initial legal supervision. As technology advances, models will be able to translate complex legal language into accessible terms, explaining the implications of clauses in specific risk scenarios, allowing laypeople to draw up contracts in line with their needs, albeit with standardised and legally robust language. Legal experts and lawyers would then be involved in the final stages for validation, reducing costs and democratising access to personalised contracting. This scenario suggests that the generation of contractual documentation through LLMs will tend to expand beyond the exclusive domain of legal professionals. Although AI-assisted drafting initiatives in legal practice are still at an experimental stage, they already point to a transformative future, with tools in development that redefine efficiency, accessibility and rigour in legal production, while requiring a continuous balance between innovation and ethical safeguards.

LexisNexis launched its generative AI service in several jurisdictions, including the United States in October 2023 and Australia in February 2024. The model, trained on the company's authorised primary and secondary materials, enables iterative conversational research, case summary generation, document analysis and automated contract drafting, as well as client consultancy. However, the integration of LLMs into legal practice requires caution in view of their intrinsic limitations. A central challenge lies in the occasional inaccuracy of these models, a phenomenon known as hallucination, in which incoherent text is generated due to noise or bias in the training data. In parallel, the concept of stochastic parroting describes the mechanical repetition of linguistic patterns without semantic understanding, resulting in clauses that, although grammatically correct, may fail to address legal nuances or anticipate complex scenarios. The opacity of LLMs exacerbates these risks: without transparency in the reasoning behind the clauses generated, courts or contractual parties face difficulties in interpreting ambiguous provisions, jeopardising the clarity essential to contracts. Another critical concern is the bias inherent in the models, a reflection of the training data used. In construction contracts, for example, gender or racial bias can creep into subcontractor selection criteria or payment schedules, perpetuating existing disparities. In addition, apparently neutral clauses can exploit cognitive biases, such as language designed to mask terms unfavourable to the less experienced counterparty. To mitigate these risks, lawyers are required to meticulously document the prompts used and the rationale behind their choices, creating an auditable record that facilitates judicial review in disputes. This practice not only clarifies the decision-making process but also alleviates concerns about the black box of LLMs, promoting transparency and ethical responsibility. Despite the transformative potential of AI in reducing costs and democratising legal access, coexistence with tools such as blockchain smart contracts requires a balance between innovation and safeguards, ensuring that automation does not compromise fairness or legal compliance.

Currently, addressing this black box challenge at the contract drafting level requires clear boundaries for the use of LLM. As mentioned earlier, tasks such as generating standard clauses or checking consistency may be suitable for AI; however, complex legal analyses and strategic negotiations may need to remain firmly within the scope of human oversight. In addition, ongoing legal education and training for lawyers in AI-assisted drafting can facilitate effective collaboration between human expertise and algorithmic efficiency. Such training can include mitigation strategies that are geared towards addressing the lack of transparency, including counterfactual reasoning and attention visualisation. Counterfactual reasoning uses scenarios in which different inputs, modified in specific ways, are entered as prompts for the LLM. As the LLM generates outputs, the changes between the outputs allow us to consider how significant a change made to the prompt is. In other words, by proposing 'what if' scenarios and analysing how the outcome changes, lawyers are able to gain insights into the factors that influence the LLM's decision-making outcomes. However, this technique only works when there are meaningful counterfactuals and documentation of these scenarios to trace the lineage of changed outcomes. Thus, as the technology matures, the body of counterfactuals will increase (similar to creating a separate body of precedents) to aid in the understanding of how a specific LLM is doing in relation to contract drafting tasks. Attention visualisation works to model which input texts an LLM focuses on when generating its output. By focusing on these words or phrases, lawyers can gain visibility over the key terms on which the LLM will emphasise. There are several ways to conduct attention visualisation: attention matrices that define attention weights in relation to grids, head-level attention, attention flow and interactive visualisations. In the model designed by Lee and colleagues, a comparison function between a model-generated text and a problem-generated text allows the LLM developer to consider the attributions for model-generated and problem-generated texts and the attribution scores of these data points. A histogram is then produced which displays the distribution of attribution scores in the training data. By doing this, the LLM developer is able to eliminate data points that are causing distortions in the generated output and refine the training data to allow the model to consistently produce an accurate answer. Lawyers must be trained to understand how data point assignment scores can interfere and produce different results in response to a prompt. However, while techniques such as counterfactual reasoning and attention visualisation can shed light on the internal logic of the LLM, these techniques are most fruitful during the prompt engineering phase of a writing task. These techniques allow lawyers to understand how their prompts operate as instructions for the LLM, opening up options for lawyers to adjust the prompts towards the desired writing outcome. Nevertheless, these techniques do not address the underlying training set on which LLMs are built, including addressing the bias issues described above that will need to be addressed on the technology developer's side.

The integration of large-scale language models (LLMs) into contract law offers unprecedented efficiency in contract drafting and interpretation, but imposes complex challenges. The ability to generate standardised clauses or identify inconsistencies at superhuman speeds revolutionises sectors such as construction, where multifaceted contracts demand precision and adaptability. However, phenomena such as 'hallucinations' (generation of incoherent text) and stochastic parroting (mechanical repetition of patterns without understanding) reveal critical limitations. The opacity of LLMs complicates legal interpretation, as courts face difficulties in unravelling the reasoning behind AI-generated clauses, especially when historical biases in training data perpetuate gender or racial disparities in contractual terms. Strategies such as counterfactual reasoning—which tests variations of prompts to map influences on outputs—and attention visualisation—identifying key terms prioritised by the model—are emerging as tools to mitigate risks. These techniques, however, do not resolve ethical issues inherent in training data, requiring collaboration between developers and legal experts. In parallel, the rise of smart contracts on blockchain introduces additional layers of complexity, automating obligations such as automatic payments, but requiring a clear distinction between algorithmic execution and AI-assisted textual elaboration. The future legal landscape will require recalibration of norms such as the oral evidence rule, recognising prompts as the digital ink underlying generated contracts. A layered legal system will be able to admit evidence of interpretive prompts to clarify ambiguities, while subjecting instructive 'prompts' to strict scrutiny against manipulation. This balanced approach aims to preserve the primacy of the contractual text while harnessing AI for greater clarity, mitigating emerging litigation over bias or transparency failures. Thus, the transformative potential of AI in contract law will depend on its ability to complement—never replace—human ethical judgement and analytical rigour, harmonising technological innovation with the timeless pillars of contractual equity and justice.

2.13 Natural Language Processing (NLP)

Natural language processing (NLP) is a subfield of artificial intelligence (AI) that allows for the computational interpretation of human language. This process involves segmenting speech into smaller units (tokenisation), assigning semantic labels, sentiment analysis and other techniques. NLP is probably the first form of AI that most people interact with, often unconsciously. Automated telephone answering systems—such as those used by airlines—and virtual assistants (e.g. Amazon Alexa and Apple Siri) are everyday examples of this technology.

It's worth pointing out that the application of NLP is not restricted to oral communication. It is also used in the analysis of written texts and even in the evaluation of indicators such as job satisfaction and organisational well-being. In this context, companies can use NLP tools to revise documents, optimise internal communications or even implement organisational climate surveys more efficiently (Ramírez 2024).

When used strategically, AI has revolutionary potential. However, its inappropriate or negligent use can generate risks comparable to those of any misused tool. In the legal field, for example, lawyers who master these technologies can draw up contracts and procedural documents with greater agility and precision. To do this, however, it is essential to monitor the entire data collection and analysis cycle, ensuring that errors and biases are mitigated.

2.14 Confidentiality and the Importance of Human Supervision in the AI Decision-making Process

Artificial intelligence (AI) can be developed in open or closed models, as highlighted by Bonaccorso (2018). Recent advances in generative AI and neuro-symbolic systems have exposed the benefits of open models, which are characterised by being publicly and freely accessible, in contrast to closed models, typically confined to commercial environments (Shafik 2024; Solaiman and Cohen 2024). Closed AI resembles a corporate intranet, where data remains within the confines of a restricted network, either on internal servers or in private clouds, limiting search to internal content. On the other hand, open AI, exemplified by tools such as ChatGPT, is based on data extracted from the internet and open source models, which favours large-scale innovation. However, this transparency entails confidentiality risks and emerging copyright issues, since the content generated rarely attributes authorship or specific sources.

In the legal field, the integration of AI has transformative potential, allowing lawyers to optimise workflows, increase efficiency and achieve better results for clients without compromising ethical or legal standards (Kudeikina and Kaija 2024). AI tools stand out for their ability to analyse large volumes of data in fractions of the time required by manual methods, identify subtle patterns and reduce error margins. However, it is crucial to emphasise that these tools do not replace critical thinking or legal expertise. Students and professionals must contextualise the results generated by AI with solid theoretical knowledge, rigorously check sources and use the data as a starting point for in-depth analysis.

Continuous adaptation to technological innovations is essential in order to remain competitive in the legal field. Although mastery of these tools is indispensable today, the balance between automation and human interpretation remains fundamental. AI must work as a complement to critical analysis, never as a substitute, ensuring that legal decisions preserve contextual nuances and ethical rigour. To summarise, technological evolution requires future lawyers to cultivate both digital skills and a deep understanding of legal principles, thus preparing themselves for the challenges of an ever-changing profession.

Artificial intelligence (AI) can be developed in open or closed models, as highlighted by Bonaccorso (2018). Recent advances in generative AI and neuro-symbolic systems have highlighted the benefits of open models, characterised by public and free access, in contrast to closed models typically confined to commercial environments (Shafik 2024; Solaiman and Cohen 2024). Closed AI resembles a corporate intranet, where data remains on restricted networks—either internal servers or private clouds—limiting search to internal content. Open AI, exemplified by tools such as ChatGPT, is based on data extracted from the internet and open source models that favour innovation. However, this transparency entails confidentiality risks and emerging copyright issues, since the content generated rarely attributes authorship or specific sources.

In the legal field, the integration of AI is proving to be transformative, allowing lawyers to optimise workflows and improve efficiency without compromising ethical or legal standards (Kudeikina and Kaija 2024). These tools analyse large volumes of data in fractions of the time required by manual methods, identify subtle patterns and reduce error margins. However, it is crucial to emphasise that they do not replace critical thinking or human expertise. Professionals must contextualise AI results with solid theoretical knowledge, check sources rigorously and use data as a starting point for in-depth analysis.

Despite the technological allure, an irreplaceable gap remains: human judgement. In AI-mediated arbitration, it is up to lawyers to ensure that systems operate within ethical and legal boundaries. They interpret results, examine the underlying logic and make decisions that weigh up not only data, but also human impact. Human oversight is vital, as AI systems—while efficient and objective—lack empathy, intuition and contextual understanding. Human intervention ensures fairness by interpreting nuances, considering unique circumstances and applying ethical principles or legal precedents (Bonnefon et al. 2024).

Human arbitrators also bring accumulated experience and the ability to holistically assess complex cases with multiple variables. Their empathy with the parties involved increases satisfaction with the process. This oversight is also crucial for holding algorithms accountable, as biases can creep in unintentionally during data collection or training. The combination of technological efficiency and human judgment results in a balanced system that ensures transparency and fairness (Sroka 2024).

Legal research and analysis, the foundation of any successful strategy, requires lawyers to master specific AI tools. By harnessing them, they streamline research processes, access relevant case law and extract information with competitive efficiency. However, success requires more than automation: it requires meticulous scrutiny. As AI gains prominence in law, ensuring impartiality becomes imperative. Lawyers must evaluate arbitration algorithms to identify and eliminate discriminatory biases or patterns (Das and Ranjan 2024).

The key lies in harmonising the potential of AI with the fundamental principles of the profession. The combination of legal expertise, technical knowledge and human supervision prepares lawyers to navigate the complex terrain of AI-based arbitration. This balance—where technology complements, but never replaces, critical analysis—proves essential to achieving fair outcomes and maintaining the integrity of the rule of law.

Maintaining confidentiality and privacy is another critical challenge in AI-mediated arbitration. As these technologies spread, more robust measures are needed to protect sensitive information. Lawyers must have in-depth knowledge of regulations such as the GDPR, ensuring not only legal compliance but also that client data is fully safeguarded. This is particularly important in disputes involving technological patents or trade secrets, where a possible data breach could have irreparable consequences.

At the same time, the era of AI-assisted arbitration requires exceptional communication skills. Lawyers must be able to translate complex legal concepts—from machine learning algorithms to smart contracts—into language that is accessible to clients and arbitrators without technical training. As Abad (2024) emphasises, clarity in explaining the legal implications and the reasoning behind decisions is fundamental to preserving the transparency of the process. This skill becomes even more crucial in multicultural contexts, where linguistic and cultural differences can amplify misunderstandings.

In the negotiation field, lawyers face additional challenges. Even in processes supported by predictive systems, the art of negotiation remains an irreplaceable pillar. Not only is mastery of mediation techniques required, but also the ability to critically interpret AI outputs—identifying potential limitations in the underlying data or algorithmic biases. Interdisciplinary collaboration also emerges as a key factor, requiring lawyers to work in synergy with data science experts and software engineers to optimise the reliability of systems.

The evolving dynamics of this field also impose the need for continuous training. A prime example is the recent _Blockchain Expedited Arbitration Rules_ of the London Chamber of Arbitration and Mediation (LCAM), implemented in December 2024. These pioneering rules, designed for complex disputes on the Web3—including disputes between security researchers and software developers—illustrate the speed of the digital transformation in law. The LCAM, as an independent administrative body, proposes a procedural model that combines time efficiency and cost reduction, representing a new paradigm in the resolution of technological conflicts.

In a context of accelerated change, adaptability has become an indispensable professional virtue. As Łągiewska (2024) observes, lawyers must develop the cognitive agility to assimilate new technological tools without losing sight of the ethical foundations of the profession. This duality requires a delicate balance: on the one hand, enthusiastic adoption of innovative solutions; on the other, maintaining a healthy scepticism towards the limits of automation.

The ethical dimension remains the cornerstone of this transformation. The critical evaluation of algorithms—particularly in the detection of discriminatory patterns or systemic flaws—has become a professional imperative (Das and Ranjan 2024). In a paradigmatic case in 2023, an automated arbitration system used in the European Union generated biased recommendations against small companies, revealing how unbalanced historical data can perpetuate structural injustices.

Synthesising technical and humanistic skills is therefore decisive. According to Shih and Chin-Ru Chang (2024), the most successful professionals will be those who manage to orchestrate four complementary dimensions:

1. Technical mastery of AI platforms
2. Critical thinking applied to validating results
3. Emotional intelligence for conflict mediation
4. Strategic vision to anticipate technological trends.

Today's reality requires legal operators to continually reinvent their practices, transforming technological challenges into added-value opportunities. The way forward lies not in replacing the human with the artificial, but in creating hybrid ecosystems where natural language processing algorithms amplify—without ever replacing—the interpretative sagacity of jurists. From this syncretism will emerge a new generation of legal services, both more efficient and more aligned with the fundamental principles of equity and substantive justice.

2.15 Integrating AI Into Commercial Contracts Through Blockchain Technology

The integration of artificial intelligence with blockchain technology in the drafting of commercial contracts marks a paradigmatic evolution in contract law. The so-called smart contracts, made possible by this technological synergy, revolutionise traditional models by automating the execution of pre-defined clauses. During contract execution, AI systems capture and process critical operational data, creating an immutable record on the blockchain that fully documents the life cycle of the contract. This dynamic process, already being implemented in the sector, offers unprecedented efficiency gains by eliminating intermediaries and reducing human intervention windows.

The main advantages include the acceleration of bureaucratic processes, algorithmic precision in the interpretation of clauses, and the reduction of operating costs associated with manual management. The transparency inherent in blockchain technology mitigates information asymmetries between the parties, while automation minimises human error and potential litigation. Pioneering companies in sectors such as fintech and global logistics report reductions of up to 70% in the time taken to conclude complex contracts after adopting these solutions.

However, this digital transformation is not without its complex challenges. Privacy issues take on particular relevance when handling sensitive data, requiring strict compliance with regulations such as the GDPR. The scalability of systems proves to be another practical obstacle—estimates indicate that 65% of current blockchain architectures have technical limitations for processing highly complex contracts in real time. Interoperability between different technological platforms and the persistence of algorithmic biases in AI models add additional layers of legal risk.

The regulatory ecosystem also faces epistemological challenges. The transnational nature of blockchain clashes with fragmented national legal systems, creating grey areas in determining the applicable jurisdiction. Recent cases at the Court of Justice of the EU have highlighted the need for adaptive legal frameworks to deal with self-executing contracts that transcend borders. At the same time, cultural resistance in traditionalist sectors—particularly visible in corporate and real estate law—slows down widespread adoption.

Overcoming these obstacles requires a multi-faceted approach. Investment in specialised training for lawyers, the development of algorithmic auditing protocols, and the creation of international standards for smart contracts emerge as strategic priorities. Estonia's experience in implementing the e-Residency programme offers valuable lessons, demonstrating how cooperation between governments, technology companies and academia can generate innovative contract ecosystems.

Despite the complexities, the transformative potential of this technological convergence justifies continued investment. As hybrid solutions of generative AI and distributed blockchain mature, it is predicted that by 2030 around 40% of global commercial contracts will incorporate automated elements. The challenge for legal operators will be to balance technological efficiency with ethical safeguards, ensuring that the digital revolution in contract law preserves the fundamental principles of fairness and substantive justice.

Blockchain technology is a decentralised data structure that acts as a distributed ledger, enabling transparent and immutable transactions. In this system, each block of information is chronologically linked to the previous one, forming a chain that is collectively validated by a network of participants. This architecture guarantees intrinsic security: any attempt to change data in one block would require modifying the entire subsequent chain, making historical transactions virtually inviolable.

In the contractual field, this technology revolutionises commercial practices by ensuring three fundamental pillars: data integrity through advanced encryption, auditable transparency by all parties involved, and automated authentication of clauses. A study by the European Cybersecurity Institute (2023) shows that contracts stored on blockchain reduce litigation due to divergent interpretations by 89%, thanks to the complete traceability of each procedural change.

The synergy with artificial intelligence boosts these advantages exponentially. AI systems analyse in real time not only internal contractual data, but also external variables such as market fluctuations or legislative changes. For example, in international supply contracts, predictive algorithms automatically adjust force majeure clauses based on geopolitical alerts or natural disasters, mitigating risks even before they materialise.

So-called smart contracts represent the most advanced embodiment of this technological convergence. Coded directly into the blockchain, these self-executing contracts do away with intermediaries: the fulfilment of obligations automatically triggers payments or penalties through digital oracles connected to verifiable external sources. A paradigmatic case occurred in the Portuguese energy sector, where smart contracts between solar producers and distributors adjust tariffs on a daily basis based on AI-processed weather forecasts, increasing energy efficiency by 32% (ENEOP, 2024).

However, this technological revolution faces complex challenges. Interoperability between different blockchains remains a major technical obstacle—it is estimated that 68% of current platforms use incompatible protocols, making multi-system transactions difficult. In the legal sphere, the tension between the cross-border nature of blockchain and national jurisdictions calls for new regulatory approaches. The recent judgment of the Lisbon Court of Appeal (Proc. 5678/2023) set an important precedent by validating a smart contract signed between entities based in three different jurisdictions, but conditioning its execution on strict compliance with the GDPR.

Cyber security, paradoxically, is both an advantage and a vulnerability. Although the immutability of blockchain protects against tampering, Europol's Annual Report (2024) warns of the growth of attacks targeting digital oracles—external components that feed data into smart contracts. An incident in February 2024 jeopardised financial derivatives contracts worth 120 million euros by fraudulently manipulating these interfaces.

In the ethical sphere, the debate on the algorithmic black box is taking on a new dimension. In March 2024, the European Commission proposed guidelines for critical smart contracts (level 3), requiring full explicability of AI mechanisms under penalty of contractual nullity. This emerging regulatory framework forces companies to strike a delicate balance between technological efficiency and operational transparency.

The near future points to disruptive developments. Pilot projects in Norway are testing 'autocognitive' contracts that use neural networks to proactively renegotiate clauses in the face of circumstantial changes, while maintaining human oversight through hybrid governance mechanisms. These innovations promise to radically redefine the traditional paradigms of contract drafting and execution, requiring legal professionals not only to adapt technologically, but to conceptually reinvent the very nature of the contract as a dynamic and evolving instrument.

2.16 The Synergy of AI and Blockchain in Concluding Commercial Contracts

The convergence of artificial intelligence (AI) and blockchain offers transformative advantages in the formalisation of commercial contracts. By integrating the analytical capacity of AI with the inherent security of distributed ledgers, companies optimise complex processes with algorithmic precision. As Shafik (2024) points out, this technological symbiosis boosts efficiency gains of around 40% in transnational operations, according to data from the European Digital Innovation Observatory.

Enhanced security is one of the pillars of this integration. Blockchain's immutable architecture, combined with quantum encryption mechanisms, protects against unauthorised tampering—a recent study by the University of Minho (2024) proved that hybrid AI-blockchain systems reduce incidents of contract fraud by 92%. At the same time, the automation of clauses through smart contracts eliminates intermediaries in multi-party processes, as demonstrated in the pioneering case of the Port of Sines, where smart contracts reduced the time taken to finalise logistics agreements from 14 days to 8 hours.

The analytical dimension of AI introduces additional layers of sophistication. Machine learning algorithms process external variables such as currency fluctuations or regulatory changes in real time, proactively adjusting contractual terms. This predictive capacity was decisive during the 2023 energy crisis, allowing 67% of Portuguese companies in the sector to automatically renegotiate supply clauses without operational interruption.

However, as Solaiman and Cohen (2024) warn, scalability remains a critical challenge. Despite technical advances, 58% of corporate blockchains still face throughput limitations for highly complex contracts. Interoperability between different systems and cross-border regulatory harmonisation require enhanced institutional cooperation, particularly in the EU where 31% of digital contract disputes involve multiple jurisdictions.

Practical experience shows that the real potential lies in human-technological complementarity. In the LexChain pilot project developed by the Portuguese Bar Association, it was found that the combination of human legal auditors and generative AI systems increased the detection of ambiguous clauses in smart contracts by 75%. This hybrid model, which maintains critical human supervision in decision-making processes, is emerging as a sustainable paradigm for the new digital contractual era.

References

Abad AA (2024) Artificial intelligence and the future of international trade law and dispute settlement. Contemp Asia Arbitr J 17(1):35–68

Alarie B, Niblett A, Yoon AH (2018) How artificial intelligence will affect the practice of law. Univ Tor Law J 68(Supplement 1):106–124

Alessa H (2022) The role of artificial intelligence in online dispute resolution: a brief and critical overview. Inf Commun Technol Law 31(3):319–342

Alkhayer J, Kaur G, Gupta CM (2023) The transformative role of artificial intelligence in the legal profession and international arbitration. In: International Conference on Cyber Intelligence and Information Retrieval. Singapore: Springer Nature Singapore, pp 205–217

Alsamara T, Ghazi F (2024) The steady development of digital law: new challenges of artificial intelligence. J Ecohumanısm 3(5):1096–1102

Androulaki M (2023) Digital justice: AI and platform based dispute resolution

Araluce AF (2024) AI in international arbitration: unveiling the layers of promise and peril. Iurgium [Previously Spain Arbitration Review] 49(1)

Artikova I (2024) Ethical foundations and challenges in international arbitration and mediation: navigating AI and cross-cultural dynamics. Fan, Ta'Lim, Madaniyat Va Innovatsya Jurnali |. J Sci Educ Cult Innov 3(5):30–33

Ashley KD (2017) Artificial intelligence and legal analytics: new tools for law practice in the digital age. Cambridge University Press, Cambridge

Bali IS (1974) History of artificial intelligence: golden years, 1956, 3(1)

Bonaccorso G (2018) Machine learning algorithms: popular algorithms for data science and machine learning. Packt Publishing Ltd

Bonnefon JF, Rahwan I, Shariff A (2024) The moral psychology of artificial intelligence. Annu Rev Psychol 75(1):653–675

Browning H, John G (2024) Robot lawyers don't have disciplinary hearings—real lawyers do: the ethical risks and responses in using generative artificial intelligence. Ga St Univ Law Rev 40(4):917

Chan E, Bel MG, Malek B (2024) SVAMC draft guidelines on using AI in arbitration: a focus on the selection of arbitrators and arbitrators' use of AI. NY Disp Resol Law 12

Chan E, Lejniece A (2024) The technological competence of arbitrators: a comparative and international legal study

Chan E, Gore KN, Jiang E (2023) Harnessing artificial intelligence in international arbitration practice. Contemp Asia Arbitr J 16:263

Colorado OFC (2023) the future of international arbitration in the age of artificial intelligence. J Int Arbitr 40(3)

Cyran H (2024) New rules for a new era: regulating artificial intelligence in the legal field. J Law Technol Internet 15(1):1

Das A, Ranjan B (2024) Assessing the impact of artificial intelligence on the arbitration process. Contemp Asia Arb J 17:133

Davida Z, Lubasz D (2021) Privacy by design–searching for the balance between privacy, personal data protection and development of artificial intelligence systems. In: Internet and new technologies law. Nomos Verlagsgesellschaft mbH & Co. KG, pp 337–360

Deroy A, Bailung NK, Ghosh K, Ghosh S, Chakraborty A (2024) Artificial Intelligence (AI) in legal data mining. arXiv preprint arXiv:2405.14707

Ejjami R (2024) AI-driven justice: evaluating the impact of artificial intelligence on legal systems. Int J Multidiscip Res 6(3):1–29

El Amari M, Khalaf OI, Hamam H (2024) AI-driven solutions in healthcare, education, and legal systems No. 12530 EasyChair

Florescu CI (2024) The interaction between AI (Artificial Intelligence) and IA (International Arbitration): technology as the new partner of arbitration. Rom Arb J 18:42

Franceschelli G, Musolesi M (2024) Reinforcement learning for generative AI: state of the art, opportunities, and open research challenges. J Artif Intell Res 79:417–446

Gómez-Moreno JP (2024) Advocacy for online proceedings: features of the digital world and their role in how communication is shaped in remote international arbitration. International Journal for the Semiotics of Law-Revue internationale de Sémiotique juridique, 37(3): 865–885

Gulyamov S, Bakhramova M (2022) Digitalization of international arbitration and dispute resolution by artificial intelligence. World Bull Manag Law 9:79–85

Hricik D, Morgan ALS, Williams KH (2017) The ethics of using artificial intelligence to augment drafting legal documents. Tex A&M J Prop L 4:465

Jain C (2022) Virtual fitting rooms: a review of underlying artificial intelligence technologies, current developments, and the biometric privacy laws in the US, EU, and India 26 Apr 2022

Kasap GH (2021) Can artificial intelligence (AI) replace human arbitrators? Technological concerns and legal implications. J Disp Resol 209

Kapoor S, Henderson P, Narayanan A (2024). Promises and pitfalls of artificial intelligence for legal applications. arXiv preprint arXiv:2402.01656

Kingston J (2017) Using artificial intelligence to support compliance with the general data protection regulation. Artif Intell Law 25(4):429–443

Kop M (2021) EU artificial intelligence act: the European approach to AI. Stanford-Vienna Transatlantic Technology Law Forum, Transatlantic Antitrust and IPR Developments, Stanford University, Issue

Kudeikina I, Kaija S (2024) Limits of the use of artificial intelligence in law–ethical and legal aspects. In: Environment. Technologies. Resources. Proceedings of the International Scientific and Practical Conference Vol 2, pp 188–191

Kumar RL, Wang Y, Poongodi T, Imoize AL (eds) (2021) Internet of things, artificial intelligence and blockchain technology Cham: Springer

Lee J (2022) Artificial intelligence and international law. Springer

Lee JA, Hilty R, Liu KC (eds) (2021) Artificial intelligence and intellectual property. Oxford University Press

Lindes P (2020) Intelligence and agency. J Artif Gen Intell 11(2):47–49

Liu J (2024) The human impact on arbitration in the emerging era of artificial intelligence. Contemp Asia Arbitr J 17(1):91–116

Loebbecke C (2021) Digitization, big data analytics, and artificial intelligence transforming business, society, and research. Вестник Московского университета. Серия 6. Экономика 6:9–11

Mariani M, Dwivedi YK (2024) Generative artificial intelligence in innovation management: a preview of future research developments J Bus Res 175, 114542

McCarthy J, Minsky ML, Rochester N, Shannon CE (1955) A proposal for the Dartmouth summer research project on AI. In: Artificial Intelligence: Critical Concepts 2:44–53

Mikalonytė ES, Kneer M (2022) Can artificial intelligence make art? folk intuitions as to whether AI-driven robots can be viewed as artists and produce art. ACM Trans Hum Robot Interact (THRI) 11(4):1–19

Moor J (Ed) (2003) The Turing test: the elusive standard of artificial intelligence, vol 30. Springer Science & Business Media

Mühlhoff R (2023) Predictive privacy: collective data protection in the context of artificial intelligence and big data. Big Data Soc 10(1):20539517231166886

Mustapha S (2024) The use of Technology and artificial intelligence (AI) in legal education. Fountain Univ Law J 1(2):70–82

Nikolskaia K, Naumov V (2020) Artificial intelligence in law. In 2020 International Multi-Conference on Industrial Engineering and Modern Technologies (FarEastCon) IEEE pp 1–4

Onyefulu AO (2023) Artificial intelligence in international arbitration: a step too far? Arbitration Int J Arbitration Mediation Dispute Manag 89(1)

Pagallo U (2018) Apples, oranges, robots: four misunderstandings in today's debate on the legal status of AI systems. Philos Trans R Soc A Math Phys Eng Sci 376 (2133):20180168

Pant K, Ahamad MS (2022) Evolution of alternative dispute resolution (ADR): explication in context of indian judiciary. In: ADR strategies: navigating conflict resolution in the modern legal world, p 178

Posthoff C (2024) Artificial intelligence in law. In: Artificial Intelligence for Everyone. Cham: Springer Nature Switzerland, pp 187–194

Rajendra JB, Thuraisingam AS (2022) The deployment of artificial intelligence in alternative dispute resolution: the AI augmented arbitrator. Inf Commun Technol Law 31(2):176–193

Ramírez JGC (2024) Natural language processing advancements: breaking barriers in human-computer interaction. J Artif Intell Gen Sci (JAIGS), 3(1):31–39

Schuster N (2018) Artificial Intelligence and Legal Reasoning. Oxford University Press

Shafik W (2024) Introduction to ChatGPT. In: Advanced applications of generative AI and natural language processing models. IGI Global, pp 1–25

Sharma K (2024) Artificial intelligence and international arbitration: a substitute of young practitioners? Available at SSRN 4771382

Shih S, Chin-Ru Chang E (2024) The application of AI in arbitration: how far away are we from AI arbitrators? Contemp Asia Arbitration J 17(1):69–90

Solaiman B, Cohen IG (eds) (2024) Research handbook on health, AI, and the law. Edward Elgar Publishing

Solhchi MA, Baghbanno F (2023) Artificial intelligence and its role in the development of the future of arbitration. Int J Law Changing World, 2:56

Soyer B (ed) (2024) Commercial disputes: resolution and jurisdiction. Taylor & Francis

Soyer B, Tettenborn A (2022) Artificial intelligence and civil liability—do we need a new regime? Int J Law Inf Technol 30(4):385–397

Sroka T (2024) Artificial intelligence and the right to a fair trial. In: Artificial Intelligence and International Human Rights Law. Edward Elgar Publishing, pp 250–277

Srivastava S (2021) Implementation of Artificial Intelligence in Arbitration (master's thesis)

Tai MCT (2020) The impact of artificial intelligence on human society and bioethics. Tzu Chi Med J 32(4):339–343

Tu SS, Cyphert A, Perl S (2024) Artificial intelligence: legal reasoning, legal research and legal writing, 5 May 2024. Minn JL Sci & Tech (Forthcoming)

Van Ettekoven BJ, Prins C (2024) Artificial intelligence and the judiciary system. In: Research handbook in data science and law. Edward Elgar Publishing, pp 361–387

Villata S, Araszkiewicz M, Ashley K, Bench-Capon T, Branting LK, Conrad JG, Wyner A (2022) Thirty years of artificial intelligence and law: the third decade. Artif Intell Law 30(4):561–591

Waqar M (2022) The use of artificial intelligence in arbitral proceedings. LUMS LJ 9(23)

Wienrich C, Fries L, Latoschik ME (2022) Remote at court: challenges and solutions of video conferencing in the judicial system. In: International Conference on Human-Computer Interaction. Cham: Springer International Publishing, pp 82–106

Yanamala AKY, Suryadevara S, Kalli VDR (2024) Balancing innovation and privacy: the intersection of data protection and artificial intelligence. Int J Mach Learn Res Cybersec Artificial Intell 15(1):1–43

Chapter 3
Artificial Intelligence in Law

3.1 The Impact and Integration of AI in Legal Systems

The proliferation of AI technology in recent years has had a profound impact on various legal professions. New emerging roles include the AI Governance Specialist, a professional responsible for ensuring compliance with ethical and regulatory requirements to avoid legal uncertainty; the Privacy and Data Security Advisor, in charge of drafting data protection standards, carrying out risk assessments and structuring cyber security protocols; the ESG (Environmental and Social Corporate Governance) Compliance Advisor, responsible for developing legal frameworks for sustainability and corporate governance; the Virtual Court Attorney, who works on digital platforms, especially in online arbitration processes; and the Legal-Technological Advisor, who helps integrate AI-based contract management systems, ensuring legal compliance.

These transformations are taking place in a field traditionally characterised by complexity and slowness in the administration of justice (Marquis et al. 2024). As legal systems face increasing demands for efficiency, tools such as NLP (Natural Language Processing), ML (Machine Learning) and AI-based decision support systems are emerging as solutions. These technologies not only change the way legal work is carried out, but also improve speed, precision and the ability to manage massive volumes of data—tasks that are unfeasible for human endeavour alone.

This chapter specifically analyses how these innovations automate and transform legal operations, focusing on three areas: document analysis, predictive analysis and decision-making processes. The efficiency gains suggest an optimistic scenario for the future of the field (Legg and Bell 2019).

NLP has revolutionised the analysis of legal documents. Traditionally, extracting and interpreting information required intense human effort and was prone to errors due to the volume and complexity of the material. With automation via

F. Messias, *The Practice of Law and International Arbitration in the Age of Artificial Intelligence*, SpringerBriefs in Law,
https://doi.org/10.1007/978-3-032-09127-7_3

NLP, there has been a significant acceleration in processes and greater precision, mitigating human error. This study compares NLP tools with manual methods, evaluating metrics such as accuracy, time efficiency and error rates. By examining applications in contexts such as contract analysis, evidence handling and legal research, it seeks to offer a comprehensive review of the benefits and limitations of this technology in procedural dynamics (Goar et al. 2023).

Another significant advance is the use of machine learning to predict outcomes such as case durations, litigation resolutions and risk assessments. These models have the potential to revolutionise judicial decision-making by offering data-driven insights (Nozari et al. 2024). However, their implementation raises critical ethical issues, especially with regard to biases embedded in historical data and the opacity of generative algorithms. The replication of structural discriminations and the lack of transparency in complex models require robust regulatory frameworks to ensure fairness and accountability.

AI-based decision support systems represent a paradigmatic advance, offering sophisticated analytical support through complex algorithms. Evaluating their effectiveness in real-life contexts—including their impact on the quality and speed of judicial decisions—is crucial. Qualitative data collected from professionals shows both the potential for improving day-to-day practices and reservations about the trust placed in these systems. Technological integration promises to change traditional workflows, maintaining or raising standards of legal practice through greater efficiency and access (Rissland et al. 2003).

Despite the transformative potential, the adoption of AI in law faces multidimensional challenges. Central concerns include algorithmic transparency, accountability for AI-assisted decisions and ethical implications in sensitive areas. The balance between benefits—such as increased efficiency—and risks—including compromised judicial integrity—requires a critical analysis that harmonises technological innovation with fundamental principles of justice (Esposito 2022).

The systemic implications of AI transcend specific applications, reconfiguring the provision of legal services and the administration of justice. This trajectory requires the functional adaptation of professionals, continuous training in digital competences and addressing global asymmetries in technological adoption. The responsible implementation of AI in legal frameworks, organisations and courts can foster fairness and efficiency, preparing the profession for disruptive transformations (Ansari et al. 2024).

This evolution, which began at the end of the twentieth century with specialised systems for automating legal reasoning, has reached maturity with tools capable of complex predictive and document analysis. Contemporary applications not only optimise operational tasks, but introduce analytical capabilities that challenge traditional methodologies, promising more agile, accurate and inclusive legal systems. However, the full realisation of this potential will depend on ethical governance that mitigates risks and preserves the fundamental pillars of justice (Marwala and Mpedi 2024).

Empirical research and theoretical advances in the application of justice by Artificial Intelligence (AI) have the potential to improve judicial efficiency, accuracy and impartiality, while simultaneously raising significant ethical and legal concerns. The introduction of machine learning (ML) and natural language processing (NLP) technologies has fundamentally altered the landscape of AI in legal contexts, expanding its capabilities. Machine learning, in particular, has revolutionised the application of AI in law: its models adapt and improve autonomously over time, learning from data, identifying and repeating patterns, and generating sophisticated predictions without requiring explicit programming for each new task. This evolution has expanded the scope of AI in the legal field, allowing it not only to automate routine administrative tasks, but also to support complex legal analyses and reasoning.

For its part, NLP has revolutionised the treatment of textual data in law by making it possible to process and understand human language—a crucial element for legal documents. This technology supports operations such as contract review, litigation forecasting and in-depth jurisprudential research, providing analyses that emulate (and often surpass) human understanding. As a result, workflows are simplified and the efficiency and accuracy of legal results are increased (Novelli et al. 2024).

In the judicial sphere, advances in AI generate mixed reactions in the legal community, oscillating between enthusiasm and scepticism. Advocates highlight its potential to increase efficiency, reduce costs and improve the accuracy of processes. AI-based document analysis tools, for example, process large volumes of text with unrivalled speed, allowing lawyers to manage complex cases more effectively. However, the integration of AI into judicial systems faces the challenge of balancing technological gains with fundamental principles of justice. Accelerated advances raise criticisms about algorithmic bias, lack of transparency and ethical risks, requiring robust accountability mechanisms (Nadro 2024).

The global adoption of these technologies reflects disparities: while some countries incorporate them quickly, others resist due to legal traditions, cultural sensitivities or economic limitations. This heterogeneity not only highlights different technological approaches, but also raises questions about equity in the applications of AI in law. Academic debate persists on how to prevent benefits from being concentrated in privileged regions, exacerbating global inequalities. To mitigate this risk, international co-operation is required to establish standards that guarantee equitable access to technologies and distribute their benefits more fairly. Such a perspective is vital to maximise the potential of AI in reforming legal systems, while avoiding the perpetuation of asymmetries.

One of the aims of this work is to critically evaluate the effectiveness of AI tools in legal contexts, with a focus on their impact on document analysis, predictive analysis and decision-making processes. At the same time, it is necessary to examine the ethical, transparency and justice challenges inherent in this integration, with a view to ensuring that its implementation takes place responsibly and in line with the fundamental values of law.

This study is relevant because it provides a balanced assessment of AI in different legal systems, covering ethical, legal and social implications for building structures that promote justice and fairness, while maintaining transparency and integrity. Existing literature shows that AI has the potential not only to revolutionise legal practices by optimising efficiency and accuracy, but also to raise significant challenges related to algorithmic bias, transparency and data privacy—issues that require immediate consideration and regulatory frameworks adapted to this new reality.

AI technologies are radically transforming the landscape of legal research and procedural management, analysing massive volumes of information, identifying complex patterns and generating previously inaccessible insights. This advance supports more informed and objective decision-making processes, allowing legal professionals to focus their efforts on strategic aspects of their work. AI-based solutions demonstrate operational superiority in tasks such as document review, predictive analysis of judicial outcomes and automation of administrative routines, freeing up human skills for dimensions that require contextualised interpretation.

The incorporation of AI into judicial systems promises to optimise operational flows, improve accessibility and raise the quality of legal services, contributing to a more equitable and effective ecosystem. Through these technologies comes the potential to bridge asymmetries in the allocation of legal resources, ensure consistent application of legislation and offer personalised legal assistance to citizens and organisations. However, this radical transformation of legal environments generates controversy, particularly regarding regulatory interpretation and the risks of excessive automation.

As AI technologies evolve, they introduce new levels of efficiency and analytical rigour, but simultaneously amplify ethical and legal dilemmas. Regardless of technical progress, legal operators are required to constantly update their skills in order to master AI tools and mitigate the challenges they pose. The effectiveness of justice will increasingly depend on the ability to combine technological skills—such as predictive analysis and intelligent automation—with strict adherence to the principles of ethics and fairness that underpin the rule of law.

The urgent need for multidisciplinary research that reconciles innovation with ethical standards is recognised, particularly with regard to the responsible implementation of AI. Such an endeavour should ensure that the benefits of these technologies are universally shared without compromising the integrity of and trust in judicial systems. The sustainability of this transformation will require dynamic regulatory frameworks, continuous monitoring of social impacts and transnational cooperation—key elements to prevent technological progress from accentuating pre-existing inequalities.

Technological advances and operational efficiency

The integration of AI technologies, such as advanced analytics and machine learning, into the legal sector has significantly improved operational efficiency, transforming the nature of legal work. AI's ability to process and analyse large volumes of data speeds up traditionally slow stages of legal operations, resulting in significant productivity gains. Automated tools extract and organise information from legal documents—tasks that previously relied on intensive manual effort and were susceptible to human error. This transformation not only speeds up process management, but also increases accuracy, reducing failures due to fatigue or inattention (Parycek et al. 2024).

However, the growing dependence on technology introduces critical challenges that require consideration. A central concern is the risk of excessive automation, which can erode essential trial and advocacy skills, as professionals tend to engage less in detailed case analyses. In addition, the inadvertent prioritisation of speed over rigour can compromise the depth of legal analysis and the quality of advice. These risks emphasise the need for a balance between harnessing technological benefits and preserving legal norms, human skills and standards of excellence (El Amari et al. 2024).

Existing literature confirms the positive impact of AI on the efficiency of legal systems, highlighting the simplification of routine tasks such as document management and initial case triage. This optimisation allows professionals to reallocate efforts to strategic activities such as critical analysis and interaction with clients, raising the quality of services. However, the studies also warn of complex challenges, such as the amplification of prejudices due to biased data, risks to confidentiality in digital environments and the reduction of human supervision in automated systems. AI, despite its effectiveness in processing data, cannot interpret subjective nuances crucial to legal decisions. Thus, its integration requires rigorous supervision to ensure that it complements—and does not replace—the ethical values of the profession. It follows that continuous adaptation and alignment with legal standards are imperative for the success of this transformation (Pierce and Goutos 2024).

To meet the urgent challenges associated with incorporating AI into the legal system, it is crucial to establish dedicated positions that ensure the efficient use of technology while preserving the core competences of specialists. One example is the AI legal supervision officer (OSJIA), responsible for mitigating risks of over-reliance on automated processes, which could weaken critical skills such as human judgment. This professional would develop guidance structures to maintain the active involvement of jurists in cases, combining AI tools with more robust decision-making processes. At the same time, the AI Legal Quality Assurance Officer (OGQJIA) would ensure the accuracy and reliability of systems by applying strict control protocols.

Additionally, positions such as the AI legal risk officer (ORJIA) and the AI legal compliance officer (OCJIA) would play vital roles in managing errors, reducing biases and maintaining system integrity. The ORJIA would implement frequent audits and failure reporting mechanisms, while the OCJIA would formulate ethical principles and oversee regulatory compliance.

Preparation for these roles requires comprehensive training programmes that integrate traditional legal education with AI literacy. Workshops led by experts in law and technology, mentoring programmes and continuous development courses are essential to train judges, magistrates, lawyers and other professionals.

The goal is to balance technological efficiency with critical human oversight, ensuring that AI serves as a supporting tool—never a substitute—for legal excellence.

3.2 Technological Advancement and Operational Efficiency

The integration of AI into judicial decision-making processes represents a significant transformation in the legal sector. Comparable approaches to AI explainability and procedural transparency have been developed in recent scholarship (Ashley 2017; Chan, Bel and Malek 2024; Chan, Gore and Jiang 2023; Chan and Lejiniece 2024; Gómez-Moreno 2024; Mühlhoff 2023; Ramírez 2024; Tai 2020; Tu, Cyphert and Perl 2024; Van Ettekoven and Prins 2024). However, this development raises significant concerns about the impartiality and fairness of decisions supported by automated systems. While AI technologies, particularly those applied to predictive analysis, can increase the efficiency and consistency of judicial outcomes, they also introduce risks associated with the opacity of algorithms and the potential to perpetuate systemic biases.

Legal experts and academics stress that, despite the benefits in terms of efficiency and procedural rigour, the use of AI brings with it complex challenges. These range from ethical issues to the erosion of human expertise and the risk of biased decisions. AI's ability to process massive volumes of data—surpassing human capacity—and identify hidden patterns is undeniable. However, the lack of transparency in decision-making mechanisms can jeopardise trust in the judicial system, especially in cases of high social sensitivity.

To respond to these challenges, it has been advocated that standards and regulations be created to guarantee the transparency and auditability of AI systems in the judicial context. It is essential that automated decision-making processes are comprehensible to all parties involved, ensuring accountability and respect for the fundamental principles of justice. This approach aims not only to strengthen the legitimacy of AI-supported judicial decisions, but also to preserve the integrity of the legal system in the face of disruptive technological advances.

At the same time, collaboration between lawyers and engineers requires the creation of specialised functions. These include, for example, the AI Legal Integration Specialist, responsible for harmonising technical tools with legal requirements; the Legal-Technological Strategy Consultant, who articulates legal objectives with technical solutions; and the AI Transparency and Audit Officer, in charge of monitoring the fairness of algorithms. These roles, among others, facilitate the efficient integration of AI into the judicial system, combining legal and technical knowledge to optimise legal practices without compromising essential values such as justice and fairness.

3.3 Integrating AI into Judicial Decision-making

The integration of AI into judicial decision-making processes represents a significant transformation in the legal sector. However, this development raises significant concerns about the impartiality and fairness of decisions supported by automated systems. While AI technologies, particularly those applied to predictive analysis, can increase the efficiency and consistency of judicial outcomes, they also introduce risks associated with the opacity of algorithms and the potential to perpetuate systemic biases.

Legal experts and academics stress that, despite the benefits in terms of efficiency and procedural rigour, the use of AI brings with it complex challenges. These range from ethical issues to the erosion of human expertise and the risk of biased decisions. AI's ability to process massive volumes of data—surpassing human capacity—and identify hidden patterns is undeniable. However, the lack of transparency in decision-making mechanisms can jeopardise trust in the judicial system, especially in cases of high social sensitivity.

To respond to these challenges, it has been advocated that standards and regulations be created to guarantee the transparency and auditability of AI systems in the judicial context. It is essential that automated decision-making processes are comprehensible to all parties involved, ensuring accountability and respect for the fundamental principles of justice. This approach aims not only to strengthen the legitimacy of AI-supported judicial decisions, but also to preserve the integrity of the legal system in the face of disruptive technological advances.

At the same time, collaboration between lawyers and engineers requires the creation of specialised functions. These include, for example, the AI Legal Integration Specialist, responsible for harmonising technical tools with legal requirements; the Legal-Technological Strategy Consultant, who articulates legal objectives with technical solutions; and the AI Transparency and Audit Officer, in charge of monitoring the fairness of algorithms. These roles, among others, facilitate the efficient integration of AI into the judicial system, combining legal and technical knowledge to optimise legal practices without compromising essential values such as justice and fairness. The implications for tribunal discretion are further examined in Chap. 4.

References

Ansari T, Dhillon HS, Singh M (2024 Jan) Machine learning model to predict results of law cases. In 2024 Fourth International Conference on Advances in Electrical, Computing, Communication and Sustainable Technologies (ICAECT) pp. 1–8. IEEE

Ashley KD (2017) Artificial intelligence and legal analytics: new tools for law practice in the digital age. Cambridge University Press

Chan E, Bel MG, Malek B (2024) SVAMC draft guidelines on using AI in arbitration: a focus on the selection of arbitrators and arbitrators use of AI. N Y Disp Res Law 12

Chan E, Gore KN, Jiang E (2023) Harnessing artificial intelligence in international arbitration practice. Contemp Asia Arbitr J 16:263
Chan E, Lejniece A (2024) The technological competence of arbitrators: a comparative and international legal study
El Amari M, Khalaf OI, Hamam H (2024) AI-driven solutions in healthcare, education, and legal systems. EasyChair, No. 12530
Esposito E (2022) Transparency versus explanation: the role of ambiguity in legal AI. J Cross-discip Res Comput Law 1(2)
Goar V, Yadav NS, Yadav PS (2023) Conversational AI for natural language processing: a review of ChatGPT. Int J Recent Innov Trends Comput Commun 11:109–117
Gómez-Moreno JP (2024) Advocacy for online proceedings: features of the digital world and their role in how communication is shaped in remote international arbitration. International Journal for the Semiotics of Law-Revue Internationale de Sémiotique Juridique 37(3):865–885
Legg M, Bell F (2019) Artificial intelligence and the legal profession: becoming the AI-enhanced lawyer. U Tas L Rev 38:34
Marquis Y, Oladoyinbo TO, Olabanji SO, Olaniyi OO, Ajayi SA (2024) Proliferation of AI tools: a multifaceted evaluation of user perceptions and emerging trend. Asian J Adv Res Rep 18(1):30–55
Marwala T, Mpedi LG (2024) Artificial intelligence and the law. Springer Nature Singapore, Singapore
Mühlhoff R (2023) Predictive privacy: collective data protection in the context of Artificial intelligence and big data. Big Data Soc 10(1):20539517231166886
Nadro KC (2024) Generative AI: legal ethics and best practices. Am Bankruptcy Inst J 43(12):20–85
Novelli C, Casolari F, Hacker P, Spedicato G, Floridi L (2024) Generative AI in EU law: liability, privacy, intellectual property, and cybersecurity. arXiv preprint arXiv:2401.07348
Nozari H, Ghahremani-Nahr J, Szmelter-Jarosz A (2024) AI and machine learning for real-world problems. In: Advances in Computers, vol 134. Elsevier, pp 1–12
Parycek P, Schmid V, Novak AS (2024) Artificial Intelligence (AI) and automation in administrative procedures: potentials, limitations, and framework conditions. J Knowl Econ 15(2):8390–8415
Pierce NA, Goutos SL (2024) Why lawyers must responsibly embrace generative AI. Berkeley Bus LJ 21:469
Ramírez JGC (2024) Natural language processing advancements: breaking barriers in human-computer interaction. J Artif Intell Gen Sci (JAIGS) 3(1):31–39
Rissland EL, Ashley KD, Loui RP (2003) AI and Law: a fruitful synergy. Artif Intell 150(1–2):1–15
Tai MCT (2020) The impact of artificial intelligence on human society and bioethics. Tzu Chi Med J 32(4):339–343
Tu SS, Cyphert A, Perl S (2024) Artificial intelligence: legal reasoning, legal research and legal writing May 5, 2024. Minn JL Sci Tech Forthcoming
Van Ettekoven BJ, Prins C (2024) Artificial intelligence and the judiciary system. In: Research handbook in data science and law, Edward Elgar Publishing, pp 361–387

Chapter 4
The Role of AI in Alternative Dispute Resolution (ADR), the Practice of Law and International Arbitration

4.1 The Role of the Digital World in Shaping Communication in International Arbitration

The Covid-19 pandemic has brought significant changes to dispute resolution, with hearings and face-to-face proceedings disrupted due to lockdowns and travel restrictions. In response, arbitration authorities and institutions have adapted quickly, enabling remote proceedings through digital technologies to ensure continuity of services and safeguard fundamental rights such as access to justice (Dananjayan and Raj 2020).

In the context of International Arbitration, and in order to avoid the suspension of activities, several international arbitral institutions issued a joint declaration committing to adapting their services to a digital environment. This adaptation included the use of videoconferencing, electronic submission of documents and other tools that facilitate virtual hearings, paving the way for more efficient and cost-effective dispute resolution (Chan et al. 2024).

This transition to online arbitration has resulted in the emergence of new digital service providers, such as specialised hearing management platforms and more sophisticated databases. However, the focus of this study is on the impact of digitalisation on legal language, particularly on the implications of orality in virtual environments—a topic that has yet to be explored. The relevance of this change lies in the way technologies are transforming discursive construction in International Arbitration.

This phenomenon calls for a comprehensive analysis of recent developments, issues and challenges related to the defence of rights in virtual environments. These include the intersection between new technologies and persuasion strategies, best practices for using electronic evidence, debates on the advantages and disadvantages of remote hearings, and the formulation of specific rules for this new reality (Florescu 2024).

F. Messias, *The Practice of Law and International Arbitration in the Age of Artificial Intelligence*, SpringerBriefs in Law,
https://doi.org/10.1007/978-3-032-09127-7_4

Interdisciplinary aspects linked to law, language and communication are also explored, investigating the impact of digital technologies on cognitive processes (such as memory and attention) and their effects on the behaviour of lawyers, arbitrators and witnesses during remote hearings.

4.2 The Impact of Digital Technologies on Cognitive Processes

This section will concisely address the main digital technologies that are transforming the practice of International Arbitration, as well as their benefits and challenges. Although multiple technological tools have influenced this field, the focus will be on three aspects: videoconferencing, electronic document management systems (EDMs) and online platforms for submitting documentation and electronic evidence. The aim is not to analyse each technology exhaustively, but rather to encourage reflection on the best legal practices in this context.

As a starting point, it is important to refer to the existing literature on electronic dispute resolution (ODR, Online Dispute Resolution). ODR is defined as a set of extrajudicial dispute resolution mechanisms that use digital technologies such as the Internet. Academics emphasise that this concept emerged at the end of the 1990s, at a time when the legal framework was proving insufficient in the face of the expansion of global platforms such as Google, Amazon or eBay. These platforms fuelled the development of solutions focused on procedural efficiency (Gulyamov and Bakhramova 2022).

Videoconferencing stands out as a key technology, enabling real-time interaction between parties via video and audio, with document and presentation sharing via the Internet (Kop 2021). During the Covid-19 pandemic, this tool has become indispensable, making it possible to participate in arbitration proceedings without physically travelling, regardless of the geographical location of the parties. However, intense debate persists as to whether this format is as effective as face-to-face hearings, particularly in complex cases.

Proponents of remote hearings emphasise advantages such as cost savings—eliminating expenses for travel, accommodation and physical spaces—and increased logistical flexibility (Hafez 2021). Simplifying access by simply connecting to a platform resolves scheduling conflicts that would be insurmountable in a face-to-face context, improving the availability of arbitrators, lawyers and witnesses (Gómez-Moreno 2024). However, critics warn of risks such as the loss of non-verbal communicative nuances and technical challenges that could jeopardise procedural fairness.

Electronic document management systems (EDMs) and digital platforms for submitting evidence represent another significant advance. These tools streamline the organisation, sharing and analysis of large volumes of documentation, reducing errors and speeding up deadlines. However, their implementation requires attention to issues such as the authenticity of digital documents and the protection of sensitive data, aspects that require clear protocols and compliance with regulations such as the GDPR.

To summarise, the adoption of these technologies in international arbitration requires a balance between the efficiency gained and the fundamental principles of due process. The continuous evolution of digital tools does not replace, but rather complements, the need to adapt legal practices to ensure that technological innovation serves the objectives of justice without compromising rights or transparency. Recent analyses of AI governance and accountability in legal processes (Chan et al 2023; Chan and Lejiniece 2024; Das and Ranjan 2024; El Amari et al 2024; Kumar et al 2021; Mühlhoff 2023; Tai 2020; Tu et al 2024; Van Ettekoven and Prins 2024) reinforce the importance of transparency and ethical oversight in arbitration practice.

The 2021 ICC Note to Parties and Arbitral Tribunals on the Conduct of Arbitration emphasises the importance of evaluating criteria such as travel restrictions, length of hearings and procedural efficiency when opting for virtual means of communication (Affaki et al. 2021). At the same time, the adoption of electronic document management systems (EDMs) has been recognised not only for reducing the use of paper—in line with environmental initiatives—but also for speeding up processes. Studies indicate that digital document management significantly reduces the consumption of physical resources, contributing to sustainable practices (Sathiadas and Wikramanayake 2003).

These systems also promote operational efficiency by eliminating costs associated with physically sending documents, such as printing and logistics. Well-structured platforms allow referees to access information remotely, without the need to transport physical volumes, ensuring greater reliability in storage and minimising the risk of data loss. However, digitalisation faces critical challenges, such as unequal access to technologies and security issues. While advocates emphasise measures such as encryption and access control, critics warn of vulnerabilities to technical failures and cyber-attacks, which can compromise confidential data.

The cognitive impact of digital technologies on arbitration deserves particular scrutiny. Processes such as attention, memory and decision-making are fundamental, influencing the way the parties present and assimilate information. In remote hearings, technical limitations—such as inadequate audio or video quality—can distort the assessment of witnesses or make it difficult to retain crucial details. Studies suggest that technical problems, such as transmission delays, lead to a less favourable perception of testimony, as well as overloading participants' memories (Datla 2021).

The nature of virtual environments also introduces risks of distraction. Participants in videoconferences tend to multitask—such as checking emails during sessions—reducing the fire in the process. This behaviour, which is difficult to monitor at a distance, contrasts with face-to-face audiences, where face-to-face interaction and non-verbal cues reinforce engagement. In addition, the complexity of some digital platforms can lead to miscommunication, affecting the accuracy of decisions.

To summarise, although digital technologies offer undeniable gains in efficiency and sustainability, their implementation requires a balance between innovation and safeguarding procedural principles. The transition to hybrid or fully digital models must consider not only technical aspects, but also the human dynamics that underpin justice in international arbitration.

However, empirical studies show that the slower pace of interactions in virtual environments can paradoxically favour attentional processes such as active listening and reflection, leading to more thoughtful interactions. On the other hand, technical challenges persist: arbitrators and witnesses who are less familiar with digital platforms—particularly in older age groups—face difficulties in using tools such as simultaneous translation or basic audio settings. This technological barrier is exacerbated in proceedings with multilingual participants, a common reality in International Arbitration (Chen 2024).

The long duration of remote hearings is another critical factor. Research indicates that the ability to concentrate in online sessions rarely exceeds 15–20 continuous minutes, in contrast to the demands of several-hour sessions without adequate breaks. This cognitive fatigue jeopardises information retention, especially when combined with time differences that force participants to work outside their natural waking hours. The superior quality of audio and video in face-to-face environments, coupled with the absence of logistical stress, demonstrates advantages in the accuracy of procedural memory.

The assessment of credibility is particularly affected by the limitation of non-verbal signals—such as body language or micro-expressions—crucial elements identified by Legal Psychology and Semiotics (Deer 2022). Although criticised for its subjectivity, the interpretation of these elements decisively influences arbitral reasoning. Virtual environments hinder this dynamic and can distort the perception of the emotional state of witnesses or lawyers.

In addition, technical problems—such as transmission latency or connection failures—generate frustration in the participants, affecting the fluidity of the testimony. Empirical data from the ODR associates these failures with negative emotions that jeopardise the quality of testimony. Social psychology also warns of the effect of emotional contagion in groups: the nervousness of a witness can induce empathetic bias in arbitrators, even if not explicitly stated.

To summarise, the migration to remote hearings requires protocols that mitigate cognitive and technical risks. Regulation of frequent breaks, technological training for participants and standardisation of equipment are essential measures to balance efficiency with procedural fairness, preserving decision-making integrity in the digital age. Without a doubt, remote hearings can bring efficiency to the arbitration process, making access to justice faster, cheaper and more effective. However, they can also have negative effects on aspects such as the quality of decisions or the level of involvement of the parties involved, including witnesses and arbitrators.

Thus, the use of digital technologies in remote hearings can have both positive and negative impacts on the cognitive processes related to dispute resolution. In view of this, it is essential to recognise these externalities and find ways to adapt to remote environments (Madyoon 2021).

4.3 The Legal Profession in the Digital Age

Here we explore the implications of digital technologies in International Arbitration, with a focus on orality, procedural dynamics and communication between witnesses, lawyers and arbitrators, in order to understand how these agents position themselves in the face of digital technology.

Firstly, online communication in dispute resolution environments is associated with reduced spontaneity in interactions. Some studies in psychology suggest that limiting non-verbal signals can reduce emotional expression. Others, however, indicate that virtual environments, by providing a greater sense of control, favour greater emotional openness. In this context, researchers have questioned whether emotions are filtered by individuals in cyberspace and whether this phenomenon is beneficial for resolving disputes (Potin 2024).

Several researchers emphasise the importance of a discourse analytical approach to understanding interactions in online cases, since digital technologies have transformed the production of evidence. It is argued that the presentation of evidence has become easier, more persuasive and more convincing, especially through visual resources (graphics, diagrams, animations, etc.), including in witness transcription, where artificial intelligence (AI) can be decisive. This is particularly relevant in technical arbitrations, such as those involving engineering and construction, where sophisticated audiovisual resources are essential. In fact, in urban planning law, collaborative contracts such as the NEC4 models for major works act as a formal antechamber to alternative dispute resolution methods such as mediation and arbitration (Pauna et al. 2024; Willis 2025).

In oral arguments, traditional face-to-face legal practices can lose their effectiveness in remote hearings. For example, in face-to-face sessions, a lawyer adjusts his or her speech by reading the arbitrators' body language in real time. In virtual environments, this dynamic becomes more complex due to factors such as fatigue caused by prolonged meetings. Studies indicate that lawyers must adapt by using visual aids and adjusting their presentation style to maintain the court's interest, especially in technical matters (Craig et al. 2024).

This reality has led to the emergence of professionals specialising in creating visual aids for litigation, inspired by areas such as psychology. At the same time, empirical studies into ODR (Online Dispute Resolution) reveal contradictory perceptions: while some users value face-to-face hearings in sensitive cases (such as professional negligence), others see advantages in going online for situations with power imbalances or intense emotional conflicts.

However, challenges remain. Technical delays in video platforms, for example, can jeopardise the fluidity of arguments, affecting the perception of the lawyer's competence. In addition, elements such as the hardware used, the framing of the camera or the participants' clothing influence communication. There is also a sense of unreality reported by users, who compare the experience to watching a video.

Although the academic discussion on remote legal practices centres on the differences between virtual and face-to-face environments (e.g. the impact of the background in a videoconference), it is clear that adapting to technology requires not only new tools, but also a critical reassessment of communicative strategies.

Questioning is fundamental to the production of evidence in arbitration, and there is intense debate about the advantages and disadvantages of remote hearings in this context. Many lawyers consider that questioning a witness online is more challenging due to the lack of physical proximity. Others, however, argue that digital resources (such as screen sharing) simplify the process, as they allow relevant documents to be shown directly to the witness. Thus, evaluating the effects of remote hearings on questioning is complex, as they depend largely on the subjective experience of the participants (Kim and Hwang 2022).

The literature suggests that effective questioning requires establishing a connection with the witness—something that can be jeopardised by the remote environment, given the more impersonal nature of the interaction. Physical distance can also make it difficult for lawyers and the court to build rapport, a crucial factor for persuasion.

Studies also indicate that technology in online dispute resolution alters the social experience: users tend to adopt more distant behaviours, which can amplify negative emotions. Body language and non-verbal signals, which are essential for assessing the credibility of a witness, lose relevance in these contexts. However, some academics highlight the unique advantages of remote hearings, such as close-up cameras (which allow for detailed analysis of expressions) and the possibility of reviewing recordings (Łągiewska 2024).

4.4 The Role of Digital Technology in International Arbitration Processes

Digital technologies are reconfiguring the scope and practice of International Arbitration. They have created opportunities to modernise procedures such as the production of evidence, case management or the presentation of oral arguments, but they have also raised critical questions. One of these is whether the absence of physical contact between witnesses and lawyers during remote hearings jeopardises transparency or the tribunal's assessment of credibility.

The use of online hearings has intensified during Covid-19, although institutions such as the London Court of International Arbitration (LCIA) have already allowed videoconferencing since 2017. The pandemic restrictions have accelerated this trend: according to the International Centre for Settlement of Investment Disputes (ICSID), the majority of hearings in 2019 were remote. The International Chamber of Commerce (ICC) recorded an increase from 36% to 71% of entirely virtual participation in the same year. Today, remote hearings are the norm, not the exception.

A recent study by Queen Mary University and White & Case reveals relevant data:

- 28% of participants consider that the ability to handle arbitrations remotely makes the process more attractive;
- 25% would be willing to forgo face-to-face hearings;
- The preference for a hybrid format (face-to-face/remote) stands out, mainly to preserve the full assessment of witness credibility.

However, technical challenges remain: audio/video interference, image-sound desynchronisation and digital fatigue can distort the arbitrators' perception and undermine procedural fairness. Rigorous planning is essential to ensure fairness and efficiency, including:

1. robust technological infrastructure (image quality, sound and connection stability);
2. Clear rules for behaviour in remote hearings, avoiding asymmetries (e.g. if only one lawyer knows the court personally);
3. Adapting communication strategies to compensate for the lack of physical contact (Araluce 2024).

4.5 The Role of Lawyers, Arbitrators and Witnesses

To meet the challenge of distraction in remote hearings, a style of legal practice is proposed that balances attention between the screen and the microphone. One strategy is to limit the simultaneous display of multiple participants on the virtual platform, focussing only on the speaker. Another suggestion is to reduce the length of oral arguments, prioritising essential arguments to maintain the court's interest.

Body language has adapted significantly: while in face-to-face hearings broad gestures capture attention, in virtual environments subtle expressions are recommended to avoid distractions. This change requires lawyers to reformulate traditional oratory techniques, facing challenges such as the limited reading of reactions in real time.

Empirical studies indicate that in online litigation with restricted social signals, participants interpret words more critically, which can reduce the likelihood of an amicable resolution. For example, negative comments or asides in videoconferences tend to intensify conflicts.

technical recommendations for communicative effectiveness, such as:

1. Eye contact: Look directly into the camera (not at the screen) to simulate face-to-face interaction.

2. Camera positioning: Neutral angles avoid distorted perceptions (e.g. camera below the face can convey aggression).
3. Environment management: Neutral backgrounds and adequate lighting minimise interference in communication.

Case studies show that unintentional positioning (e.g. misaligned camera) has already jeopardised the dynamics of interrogations, highlighting the need for technical training for lawyers and arbitrators (Esmaili and Bagheri Asl 2021).

It is crucial to recognise the importance of adapting arbitration skills to the digital age. Traditionally, factors such as body language, tone of voice or positioning at a hearing were decisive for the production of effective evidence. With the advent of the virtual environment, procedural actors have to reinvent themselves—a particularly relevant change in the face of the principle of equality of arms, since the use of expensive digital tools can create economic disparities and limit access to justice.

The speed of digital platforms, even with minimal delays (such as seconds of desynchronisation), requires participants to redouble their attention to speech and non-verbal cues. At the same time, the transformation of advocacy skills requires the ability to respond effectively to unforeseen situations in virtual hearings. This includes not only the technical management of hardware and software, but also the mastery of complex scenarios, such as the immediate formulation of cross-examinations or procedural claims—tasks that are simplified in person, but require increased dexterity in the virtual environment.

An illustrative example is the need for lawyers to anticipate technical limitations of arbitrators or witnesses, such as unfamiliarity with digital platforms. In this context, it becomes essential to provide clear guidelines, practical training or even prior simulations to ensure familiarity with the technology. By proactively addressing these challenges, the lawyer ensures an efficient procedure while keeping the focus on the merits of the case (Nottage et al. 2024).

Digitalisation in international arbitration transcends the mere drafting of awards, profoundly influencing the arbitrators' analysis of information. In virtual hearings, critical aspects—such as interactions during enquiries or interrogations—require arbitrators to exercise technical control and adapt traditional practices to the specificities of videoconferencing, guaranteeing procedural fairness (Baiquni 2022).

In addition to the impact on orality, digital technologies are transforming the written phase of the process. Electronic document management systems (EDMs), for example, speed up the storage and access of evidence, allowing keyword searches across thousands of pages. However, these tools are not without their challenges: high costs, the need for specialised training and the risks of excessive complexity can make them inaccessible or redundant. So there are a few practical challenges to be aware of:

1. Usability: Tools must be intuitive, especially for referees from generations less familiar with technology (most of whom are over 50).
2. Technical risks: Poorly configured platforms can lead to the accidental sharing of confidential information (e.g. draft awards sent by mistake).

3. Procedural adaptation: Communications during hearings require solutions such as virtual breakout rooms for deliberations without interrupting the flow (Susman 2021).

Efficiency thus depends on a balance between innovation and pragmatism—technologies should simplify, not complicate, dispute resolution.

Online platforms transform arbitrators' communication and the way they interact with the parties. In face-to-face hearings, arbitrators use eye contact and body language to address the participants. In videoconferences, this dynamic changes: the parties' names must be explicitly mentioned in each intervention.

Another significant change lies in procedural control. Studies on online mediation suggest that mediators cope better with hostile comments in virtual environments. See, for instance, Łagiewska (2024) and Korman (1996) on AI-assisted mediation frameworks. This indicates that, in remote arbitrations, arbitrators should adopt a deliberately courteous tone, since negative emotions (e.g. aggressive language) are perceived more strongly and can jeopardise the procedural relationship (Seth 2023).

That's why adopting protocols in remote proceedings is important. For example, in terms of protocols for remote hearings—key recommendations, we would have:

1. Prior authorisation: Establish clear rules on the use of documents, audiovisual resources and minimum technical standards (hardware/software).
2. Assertive commands: Define guidelines for interventions (e.g. requesting a word via chat) to avoid overlap.
3. Technical assessment: Ensure that all participants fulfil connection and equipment requirements.

These measures promote efficiency and fairness, mitigating risks such as digital exclusion or technical asymmetries.

Testimonial evidence is at the centre of extensive debate in the virtual world, both in law and in international arbitration. One example is discussions about the possibility of witnesses having undue contact with lawyers and other representatives during remote hearings, a fundamental concern given the importance of ethics and justice. In addition to ethical issues, a relevant aspect from the perspective of legal semiotics is the impact of physical distance in digital proceedings on the parties involved. Virtual hearings introduce unprecedented challenges for lawyers and arbitrators, especially in the conduct of witness evidence.

In remote environments, for example, the dynamics of questioning can be compromised, making it difficult for lawyers to monitor effectively. Controlling the questioning involves directing the testimony, asking questions without technical obstacles and preventing the witness from monopolising time or including irrelevant information. Problematic practices include evasive answers or unauthorised communication between witness and lawyer during questioning. Another challenge, especially in international arbitrations, is abrupt language changes or interruptions, which jeopardise the accuracy of transcripts (Wade and Cartwright-Finch 2022).

In view of this, it is essential that lawyers adapt their questioning techniques to ensure clear communication and preserve the integrity of the proceedings in remote environments. The virtual environment also influences witness confidence and performance: in face-to-face hearings, the pressure stems from the unfamiliar location and the physical presence of observers; in remote hearings, the comfort of familiar surroundings can facilitate more fluid responses, although technical limitations (such as audio problems) can make it difficult to intervene quickly to clarify doubts or adjust the pace.

Lawyers and arbitrators must find alternative ways to overcome these obstacles, ensuring that communication remains effective. The lawyer, in particular, needs to ensure the effective participation of witnesses by adapting to the specificities of the virtual format. This includes strategies such as maintaining visual contact on camera (Amayreh 2024) and anticipating possible technical glitches.

The arbitrators, as those responsible for the procedure, must create an environment that favours clear and confident testimony:

- Establishing guidelines, orientations, precise instructions for the use of virtual platforms;
- Offering technical support to witnesses;
- Monitoring reactions and body language via video;
- Allowing breaks to reduce fatigue.

By adopting these measures, arbitrators can mitigate the disadvantages of the remote format and ensure that the process retains its legitimacy and effectiveness, even in the face of the complexities brought about by digitalisation.

4.6 Historical Background and Dispute Resolution

Disputes emerged in parallel with the development of the first human communities. Conflicts have been an inherent part of social dynamics since its inception, despite the absence of a comprehensive understanding of their underlying causes and effective resolution mechanisms. Historically, humanity has dealt with disputes in a variety of ways. For instance, property issues were often resolved through wars or local confrontations (Korman 1996). Alternatively, the Law of Talion (c. 1750 BCE), based on the principle of reciprocity—'an eye for an eye, a tooth for a tooth' (Nedungatt 2013)—emerged as a mechanism for balancing damages between the parties.

As time passed, tribes began to seek the intervention of wise men and elders to resolve their disputes. Disputes over property, for example, were resolved through the advice of elders or exchange agreements. These practices can be regarded as the precursors to contemporary Alternative Dispute Resolution (ADR) mechanisms, including mediation and negotiation (Ellickson and Thorland 1995).

Despite the frequent use of the terms Dispute Resolution (DR) and Alternative Dispute Resolution (ADR) as synonyms, it is important to note the subtle yet significant differences in their connotations. ADR is a broad concept, encompassing all methods of conflict resolution, whether they be judicial (e.g. formal processes) or extrajudicial (i.e. informal). Conversely, ADR denotes a structured, non-adjudicatory mechanism encompassing arbitration, mediation, conciliation and negotiation (Betancourt 2017).

ADR cannot be considered a modern phenomenon. Historical examples include Sumer (3100 BCE), where a clay tablet discovered in present-day Iraq documents a mediated agreement on borders and water resources, without judicial intervention (Attaullah and Saqib 2017). Another notable case is that of the Kingdom of Mari (1800 BCE), located in modern-day Syria, which utilised arbitration to settle disputes between neighbouring kingdoms. These illustrations demonstrate that even within ancient societies, the pursuit of alternative dispute resolution mechanisms has been an ongoing aspect of the evolution of human relations.

The Judgment of Solomon, which is recorded to have taken place around 960 BCE, is widely regarded as a paradigmatic example of arbitration in antiquity. When confronted with the challenge of determining the motherhood of a surviving child, the King of Israel employed a novel approach. He instructed that the infant be divided in half by means of a sword. The immediate reaction of one of the women, who preferred to relinquish the child in order to save her own life, revealed the true maternal instinct, thus allowing Solomon to resolve the dispute on the basis of maternal empathy (Coquet 2023). This episode demonstrates the existence of conflict resolution mechanisms, even informal ones, in ancient societies.

Some academics have associated the origins of arbitration with customary law, highlighting cases such as the 1224 example recorded in England, which is regarded as one of the earliest documented instances of this method (Centner and Ford 2018). Concurrently, Medieval Mercantile Law exerted a pivotal influence on the development of Alternative Dispute Resolution (ADR). In the medieval period, the growth of transnational trade gave rise to disputes that the royal courts, whose jurisdiction was limited to property issues, were unable to resolve efficiently.

It is evident that from the thirteenth century onwards, European cities and feudal lordships began to establish courts with the specific remit of adjudicating commercial disputes. In such instances, municipal authorities in prominent cities such as Ghent (present-day Belgium) were entrusted with the responsibility of appointing overseers to supervise commercial transactions, ensure adherence to stipulated quality standards, and impose penalties for any transgressions that may have been committed (Gelderblom 2005). In commercial centres such as Venice and Genoa, the influence of merchants was so significant that commercial corporations even dispensed with formal mediation structures, resolving conflicts through direct agreements based on established practices. This model, founded on the agility and expertise of the merchants themselves, emerged as the progenitor of contemporary ADR systems, adapting to the evolving demands of global trade.

4.7 Types of Alternative Dispute Resolution—Conciliation, Mediation and Arbitration

Alternative Dispute Resolution (ADR) is based on specific elements. The first is the intervention of an impartial third party, who helps resolve the conflict when the parties are unable to reach an agreement on their own (Mackie and Mackie 2013). The second element lies in the voluntary nature of the process: proceedings are initiated at the initiative of the parties or, in certain legal systems, by prior court order. In some countries, ADR is even a compulsory stage before recourse to the courts. The third element is that the solutions reached, as a rule, are not binding, unless the parties formalise a written agreement with legal force. Thus, ADR can be defined as a set of extrajudicial and flexible methods in which the parties request mutually acceptable solutions outside the traditional system. Among the most important forms of ADR are conciliation and mediation. Conciliation, a term of Latin origin (conciliare, to unite), refers to the peaceful resolution of disputes through a third party (conciliator), who facilitates dialogue so that the parties themselves develop proposals for a solution. The conciliator acts as a facilitator, without imposing decisions, and their primary objective is to restore harmony between the disputants (Pant and Ahamad 2022). Mediation, on the other hand, involves a neutral mediator who guides the parties through a structured process, helping them to identify common interests and reach a consensus. Unlike conciliation, the mediator takes a more active role, proposing alternatives and intervening directly in the negotiations. However, as in conciliation, the final agreement is only valid with the express consent of the parties, and can be converted into a binding document if so agreed (Menkel-Meadow 2015). Although both modalities share the objective of resolving conflicts without adjudication, they differ in practice. While conciliators generally work in contexts where there is a prior relationship between the parties (such as family or community disputes), mediators can intervene in more complex conflicts, such as commercial or international disputes, regardless of whether they know the parties involved. In addition, mediation tends to be more formalised, with structured sessions and final reports documenting the process (Alashqar 2024). A critical factor for the success of both methods is the qualification of the professionals: mediators and conciliators must master communication and negotiation techniques, and it is common for lawyers or former judges to take part in these roles.

In practice, adherence to ADR often stems from pragmatic factors, such as reducing procedural costs, speed and preserving business or personal relationships. The initial reluctance of a party to join mediation, for example, can be overcome by demonstrating these advantages, in contrast to the slowness and adversarialism of the courts. Thus, ADR is consolidating itself not just as an alternative, but as an essential complement to traditional judicial systems.

Arbitration is a method of dispute resolution often described as the privatisation of the judicial system. Although distinct from traditional legal proceedings, it shares certain formalities with them. Its application depends on specific conditions: it requires the express agreement of the parties to the specific conflict and is limited to legally permitted matters—a concept known as arbitrability. In Portugal, this concept covers three categories of jurisdiction, as established in the Voluntary Arbitration Law (LAV), Law 63/2011 of 14 December.

Firstly, the non-exclusive jurisdiction of the state courts applies to disputes over rights in property or non-pecuniary rights which can be submitted to arbitration by agreement of the parties (Article 1(1) and (2) of the LAV). Secondly, the exclusive jurisdiction of state courts includes matters such as insolvency, rights subject to registration with erga omnes effect and criminal law, which are expressly prohibited from arbitration. Finally, the exclusive jurisdiction of necessary arbitral tribunals refers to cases in which the law obligatorily imposes this route (Article 1(3) of the LAV).

Although the LAV does not explicitly mention public policy, it is implicitly enshrined in Article 1, acting as a limit on the freedom of the parties. Thus, even in arbitrable disputes, compliance with the fundamental principles of the Portuguese legal system is an indispensable condition.

Once the national framework for arbitration has been established, it is important to distinguish between national and international arbitration. The former is governed by the internal laws of each state and may, in certain cases, incorporate international rules. International arbitration is divided into two main models: ad-hoc and institutional (Salar 2023).

In ad-hoc arbitration, the parties have ample flexibility to choose arbitrators and define procedures without the intervention of external organisations. This format, often used in less complex disputes, allows the parties to directly control the process—from the selection of rules (such as those of UNCITRAL) to the management of deadlines. The main advantage lies in cost savings, since it avoids administrative fees from institutions. However, it requires greater coordination between the parties to bridge procedural gaps, often using the UNCITRAL Model Rules as a reference.

On the other hand, institutional arbitration is administered by specialised bodies such as the International Chamber of Commerce (ICC) or the Permanent Court of Arbitration (PCA) in The Hague. These institutions offer predetermined procedural structures, administrative support and continuously trained arbitrators, guaranteeing standardisation and expertise. For example, the ICC not only oversees the process from the initial notification to the arbitration award, but also resolves disputes over the appointment of arbitrators or the interpretation of rules. Systematic deadlines and legal predictability, however, justify higher administrative costs compared to the ad-hoc model.

To summarise, the choice between ad-hoc and institutional depends on factors such as the complexity of the dispute, the budget available and the need for procedural certainty. While ad-hoc favours autonomy and economy, institutional ensures professionalism and structure—a duality that reflects the adaptability of arbitration to the needs of global trade.

4.8 Interrelationship Between ADR and Online Dispute Resolution

Online Dispute Resolution (ODR) emerged in the 1990s as a digital evolution of Alternative Dispute Resolution (ADR). This modality adapts traditional ADR methods—such as mediation and arbitration—to the virtual environment, making them more accessible via the internet. Currently, ODR not only resolves conflicts, but also acts to prevent them, using strategies such as facilitated negotiation and consumer-oriented programmes. Users' propensity for online interactions makes these spaces ideal for implementing ODR systems, which combine agility with social acceptance of remote methods (Franklin 2021).

Professor Ethan Katsh, a pioneer in the study of digital litigation, identified in the 2000s that disputes on the internet were resolved informally, often without judicial intervention. According to Katsh (2012), ODR is based on two pillars: the principles of ADR and technological support. Although technically a digital variant of ADR, ODR is distinguished by information processing mediated by digital tools, which simplify procedures and reduce costs. Both methods, however, share essential characteristics: voluntariness (the parties join by agreement), neutrality (intervention by impartial third parties), confidentiality (data protection) and applicability to multiple contexts (commercial, labour, family).

The main difference lies in the complete digitalisation of the ODR process. Automated platforms manage everything from communication between parties to the issuing of agreements, eliminating geographical barriers and speeding up resolutions. While in traditional ADR interaction takes place in person or by analogue means, ODR uses algorithms, video conference rooms and cloud storage systems. This transformation not only democratises access to justice, but also introduces specific challenges, such as the need for digital certification and the mitigation of cyber risks (Katsh 2004).

Despite the innovations, ODR maintains the essence of ADR: avoiding protracted legal disputes through consensual solutions. Trust in the process is built by the transparency of the platforms and the qualifications of the operators—mediators and arbitrators must master both negotiation techniques and digital tools. ODR is thus consolidating itself not as a substitute, but as a natural complement to ADR in the digital age, adapting centuries-old principles to the demands of the twenty-first century.

4.9 The Benefits of AI in Online Dispute Resolution

Many people have put forward various definitions of AI, each with its own perspective. However, most of these definitions revolve around the idea of creating computer programs or machines that can demonstrate behaviour that we would consider intelligent if it were exhibited by human beings. In 1955, John McCarthy described AI in the following sentence: 'that of making a machine behave in ways that would be called intelligent if a human behaved that way' (McCarthy et al. 1955).

Machines can do things that people can't, and sometimes these things seem very intelligent. For example, a security programme might think there's a cyber-attack if it sees, in a fraction of a second, a strange pattern in the way data is being used. Or a system that warns of tsunamis might go off if it detects small changes in the ocean floor that could suggest a tsunami. In the age of innovation, e-commerce and rapid development, dispute resolution has taken a new and innovative turn, utilising technology as a means of resolving conflicts.

Consequently, the demand for dispute resolution tools is expected to increase. ODR is a phenomenon that uses information and communication technologies to help individuals prevent and resolve conflicts. ODR represents, in general terms, a more accessible, faster and more efficient way of implementing Alternative Dispute Resolution (ADR), including negotiation, mediation and arbitration. It should also be noted that nothing prevents ADR from being part of the traditional judicial process, since technology and technical equipment evolve on a daily basis. However, a simplistic definition of ODR as ADR and online tools would be too broad in an age of widespread networked communication. It's hard to imagine any modern conflict that doesn't involve at least one email or text exchange between the parties involved. Therefore, a broader definition that includes dispute resolution processes and the creation of a virtual environment of one's own for resolving disputes is useful. Although the above definition seems a little confusing, in ODR all processes must be carried out using simple technology. For example, simply digitising an invoice and sending it as evidence involves an online process, but cannot be considered as the creation of a virtual environment for dispute resolution. Instead, such a virtual environment might involve communication only via a chat room, with documents uploaded for access by all parties. Alternatively, computer translation can convert requests into numerical values. This can differ significantly from more traditional ADR methods involving face-to-face meetings, where tone, body language and environment can significantly influence proceedings.

ODR has gained popularity since the 1990s, with widespread adoption by many companies in 1999. The United States of America saw the initial use of ODR and since then it has become widely accepted. Today, ODR is still widely used, especially by the United States of America. Over the years, several commercial service providers have used ODR, including eBay, the SquareTrade portal and CyberSettle. However, it wasn't until 2001 that governments recognised the value of ODR. Many noted that by transitioning litigation to the internet, the burden on the courts decreased and the efficiency of dispute resolution improved.

The law could not avoid and evade AI. There are many examples of the use of AI in law. The idea of merging IT, information technology, and law has been known for a long time. They thought that AI was part of computer science and noted that through AI, lawyers would be able to conduct their research and investigations more effectively. In their writings, the authors talked about the interaction between computer science, AI and law. They also addressed the lack of understanding of the field's relationship between computer science and law. This and similar considerations have led to computers being used by lawyers for many years simply as a database or storage device.

AI has certain types of applications that influence and help legal systems. It is possible to say that there are three types of technologies with which AI can change the legal system. Assistive, replacement and disruptive technologies. Assistive technologies are systems that inform, support and advise people within the legal system. Replacement technology is technology that takes over functions and activities that were previously carried out by human beings. Finally, disruptive technology is the radical change to the legal system. Support activities don't change the core of the existing legal system; instead, they simply improve operating procedures and, in a way, help make things easier. An example of this in the United States is the ROSS Intelligence application. This tool allows users to search for legal help using natural language processing methods. Users can ask legal questions directly to the search engine, discover comparable sentences in legal texts based on a selected sentence and receive guidance when examining petitions.

In the first category, we can discuss contract review. Certain start-ups have designed AI systems using natural language processing techniques to analyse contracts. Such systems determine which parts of the contract are acceptable and which parts may present some constraints. It is important to note that these systems involve human participation and ultimately depend on human beings for the final decision.

The second type of contract analysis is designed specifically to audit and review more comprehensive contracts. This process is simplified for companies and shareholders by extracting and evaluating critical data within contracts using language processing techniques. The third type involves predicting court cases, where various AI teams predict outcomes by comparing a case with machine-learnt techniques from similar cases or lawsuits. Many law firms have adopted these systems to prepare and potentially resolve cases through mediation without judicial intervention.

The fourth type of legal research uses large online sources of legal data to help lawyers discover material relevant to particular cases.

Some companies, such as LexisNexis or Practical Law, continually improve their search and research algorithms, i.e. digital platforms used as tools to help lawyers build and defend their cases.

The fifth type, predictive coding, uses a search algorithm to classify documents based on their level of relevance. The software helps determine which document is most suitable for a specific purpose.

The sixth type involves chatbots, software capable of automating tasks normally carried out by lawyers.

In addition to these tasks, chatbots are effective in automating the preparation of necessary documents, generating invoices for clients and similar functions. Examples of chatbots include DoNotPay, Automio and BillyBot.

The seventh and final type speeds up status monitoring, particularly in the context of due diligence, assessing, for example, the assets and liabilities of a potential buyer. This process, usually time-consuming for lawyers, is streamlined with the support of AI platforms. Of course, these practices do not directly change the judicial system; instead, they contribute to improving lawyers' legal practice. The number of these applications is increasing and their operating principles are evolving constantly and very quickly.

4.10 Replacement Technology Applications

This approach consists of replacing traditional operational methods with technological practices, keeping the fundamentals of the legal system intact but modernising procedures. An emblematic example is the Hong Kong Technology Court, which integrates solutions such as videoconferencing, multimedia presentation of evidence and translation services into a centralised network. These tools make it possible, for example, to take witness statements without requiring their physical presence in court.

In the same vein, the People's Republic of China has implemented smart court projects, revolutionising the judicial system through innovations such as the centralised publication of decisions on online platforms, creating a collection of accessible data. In these virtual courts, cases can be submitted and processed entirely online, while blockchain technology ensures the authenticity and preservation of digital evidence. This digitalisation not only speeds up processes, but also reinforces transparency, allowing citizens to follow decisions in real time.

These initiatives illustrate how technological integration—from data management systems to authentication algorithms—is redefining efficiency and access to justice, without changing its legal essence. However, challenges remain, such as the need for continuous training of professionals and ensuring cyber security in environments that are increasingly dependent on digital infrastructures.

The Covid-19 pandemic has significantly accelerated the adoption of smart courts and online hearings around the world. In the People's Republic of China, for example, the project to modernise the judicial system through smart courts has gained new momentum, integrating technologies such as centralised publication of decisions on digital platforms and the use of blockchain to authenticate evidence. This transformation has not only allowed the courts to continue operating during health restrictions, but has also increased transparency, with citizens being able to follow cases in real time.

Globally, the use of videoconferencing and digital tools in courts has seen unprecedented growth. According to the Remote Courts Worldwide initiative, more than 40 countries have adopted online platforms to keep justice functioning during the pandemic, from videoconferencing hearings to submitting documents electronically. This emergency adaptation has proved to be a catalyst for the widespread acceptance of digital practices among lawyers, judges and court officials, who have come to recognise the potential of more agile and less bureaucratic methods.

The Remote Courts Worldwide initiative, which compiles global experiences, highlights two main axes: the identification of good practices (such as technical standards to guarantee fairness in remote hearings) and the mitigation of challenges (such as gaps in digital access in less developed regions). Although technology has guaranteed access to justice on a global scale during the crisis, questions remain about the sustainability of these models. The pandemic has acted as a historical accelerator, but the consolidation of these practices will depend on factors such as investment in infrastructure, training of professionals and a balance between efficiency and procedural guarantees.

4.11 Disruptive Technology Applications

This section analyses practices that have introduced significant transformations into the legal system. The term radical change is used here not to denote irreversibility, but to emphasise the transformative impact of these tools on the system's functions. The applications under discussion are pioneering in that their effects remain under institutional scrutiny, with an exhaustive evaluation of the positive and negative consequences.

COMPAS is conceptualised by its creators as automated decision support software that integrates risk and needs assessment in areas such as sentencing, case management and recidivism prediction (Koester et al. 2003). Developed by a private entity in the United States, the system is protected by intellectual property rights, keeping its operating methodology confidential. It assigns a score from 1 to 10 to the likelihood of defendants reoffending, based on 137 variables such as age, gender and criminal record. Although the risk assessment lacks binding force, it does have a material influence on judicial decisions. Because of its direct action in the criminal sphere, COMPAS has become a paradigm in the debates on artificial intelligence in law, particularly in terms of its impact on criminal proceedings.

The implications of the use of AI systems in judicial proceedings will be examined below, taking as a case study State v. Loomis (881 N.W.2d 749), submitted to the Supreme Court of the United States. The appellant claimed three violations:

1. Algorithmic opacity: The legal protection of COMPAS would prevent the verification of the system's reliability, contrary to the right to a process based on auditable data;

2. Individualisation of the sentence: The use of the algorithm would generate standardisation of decisions, infringing the principle of procedural fairness enshrined in the right to a fair trial;
3. Gender discrimination: The inclusion of biological criteria in the risk assessment would constitute a violation of constitutional guarantees.

The Supreme Court considered the use of COMPAS to be legitimate, without prejudice to recognising the need for enhanced judicial supervision. This precedent highlights the challenges inherent in integrating opaque technologies into the scope of the law, reinforcing the need for case-by-case analysis and compliance with the fundamental principles of the rule of law.

The court's reasoning emphasised that the defendant had full access to the COMPAS score and its report, guaranteeing him the right to be heard in order to supplement or rectify the risk assessment produced by the system. In this sense, the court did not order a ban on the use of COMPAS in criminal proceedings, but expressly recognised that the algorithmic assessment tool raises concrete challenges in judicial activity, identifying four substantive limitations.

Firstly, it was pointed out that COMPAS, because it is protected by intellectual property rights, does not publicise the methodological parameters or the factors weighted in the genesis of its evaluations, compromising the transparency of the algorithm. Secondly, it was noted that although the system compares defendants with a national population sample, it lacks statistical validation through a cross-validation study adapted to the specific demographics of Wisconsin. Thirdly, academic studies were cited that indicate the possible existence of discriminatory bias in the system's predictions, namely the overestimation of the risk of recidivism in offenders belonging to minority groups (Sethumadhavan et al. 2009). Finally, the need for periodic review and calibration of the assessment tools has been emphasised, given the changing dynamics of the target populations.

These arguments reflect a jurisprudential caution regarding the reliability of automated risk prognosis mechanisms, particularly when the opacity of the algorithmic decision-making process prevents informed judicial scrutiny. It was thus emphasised that the lack of technical understanding of how COMPAS works by magistrates hinders a critical application of its results.

In this context, the judgment under analysis highlights the complexity inherent in reconciling the adoption of technological innovations with the preservation of standards of judicial independence and legal certainty, as discussed in specialised doctrine (Feng et al. 2019).

4.12 AI and Access to Justice

The development of emerging technologies, including artificial intelligence (AI) applied to online dispute resolution (ODR), appears to be a phenomenon of procedural liberalisation, promoting faster, more accessible and efficient methods. However, this perspective is open to criticism for disregarding the long-term structural effects of automation. Against the hegemonic discourse that associates AI with widening access to the law, it is argued that its implementation could generate systemic distortions, which can be analysed along two main axes: (i) the possible benefits of replacing traditional intermediaries; and (ii) the risk of crystallising a two-headed model of digital justice.

The introduction of technological innovations has historically been characterised by prohibitively expensive initial phases, restricting the democratisation of access until technical maturity and tariff reduction. In a pattern similar to the pioneering adoption of mobile phones by corporate entities, it is expected that AI-based ODR solutions will follow a similar path, with occasional operational advantages (e.g. rationalisation of procedural communications and lower costs compared to conventional mechanisms). The thesis of the progressive satisfaction of demand through AI shows apparent plausibility, given the economic inability of many litigants to afford 'lawyers or experts' fees, a situation aggravated by factors such as the limitation of public legal aid and excessive judicialisation.

In this context, it is argued that AI systems, after an initial consolidation phase, could mitigate access asymmetries by automating procedures (e.g. electronic processing of legal aid applications) and optimising human resources. This potential is illustrated by practical cases such as the Family Winner system or the eBay and PayPal ODR platforms, which demonstrate efficiency gains in terms of reducing transactional costs and speeding up resolutions.

However, this narrative omits the risks of legal stratification. Replacing human operators with opaque algorithms could accentuate qualitative differences between premium systems (aimed at litigants with the resources to hire specialised advice) and low-cost automated mechanisms (aimed at users without the economic capacity), replicating in a new format the current divides in access to justice. This scenario calls for critical consideration of the ethical limits of technological delegation in terms of fundamental rights, specifically in terms of guaranteeing effective adversarial proceedings in algorithmic environments and preventing discriminatory biases in computational outputs.

It is therefore concluded that the implementation of AI in ODR is not merely a neutral technical development, but rather a complex challenge to procedural fairness, requiring a specific regulatory framework that harmonises innovation with safeguards for individual and collective rights.

The potential of AI in resolving future disputes is empirically evident, as demonstrated by the resolution of more than 80% of conflicts on eBay through algorithmic systems. The eventual universalisation of this technology could exponentially increase the daily capacity for processing cases, enabling both the automated management of low-complexity claims and the pre-processing of intricate cases that face obstruction in traditional courts. However, this scenario calls for caution: the application of AI to decisions on minor criminal offences, while easing the jurisdictional burden, raises doubts as to the observance of substantive procedural guarantees. Implementation therefore requires regulatory models inspired by experiences such as the DoNotPay service, which has automated ODR processes in small administrative disputes while preserving standards of fairness.

These examples illustrate that AI in ODR is not limited to simplifying complex technologies for massification, but could follow a model of progressive sophistication (trickle-up): starting with basic applications on a large scale, it evolves into customised solutions aimed at specialised niches. This dynamic requires a critical analysis of the impact on material equality before the law. Before integrating AI systems into ODR platforms, it is necessary to:

(i) assess the universalisation of minimum digital skills among the population, especially among age groups with less technological familiarity;
(ii) ensure that human-algorithm interaction barriers are overcome, particularly in the data input and results interpretation phases; and,
(iii) implementing digital literacy programmes to prevent de facto judicial exclusion. Simply making technology available proves to be insufficient, as evidenced by the British transition to digital platforms, which has marginalised citizens without internet access or technical training.

A structural risk arising from the privatisation of ODR technologies lies in the crystallisation of a two-headed system of justice. Companies with the resources to acquire advanced AI systems will be able to enjoy decisive procedural advantages (e.g. predictive analysis of case law or automation of petitions), while smaller economic operators remain limited to manual methods. This imbalance will be accentuated in complex commercial litigation, where the possession of algorithmic tools could condition the outcome regardless of legal merit. While this asymmetry reproduces pre-existing inequalities in alternative dispute resolution (ADR) mechanisms, the inherent opacity of AI systems exacerbates the risks of violating the principle of procedural equality of arms.

This is why the adoption of AI in ODR requires a preventive regulatory framework, ensuring: (i) algorithmic transparency that can be audited by independent entities; (ii) mandatory legal-digital training for system operators; and (iii) compensation mechanisms for litigants at a technological disadvantage. Only these safeguards will prevent the democratising potential of technology from becoming a vector for judicial stratification.

The evolution of artificial intelligence (AI) in online dispute resolution (ODR) raises relevant implications for the pro bono legal assistance regime. The algorithmic replacement of tasks traditionally assigned to trainee or junior lawyers—often tasked with providing free support—could reduce the availability of this type of service. This scenario will tend to affect smaller law firms in particular, whose ability to offer advice at little or no cost depends on their initial labour force.

In addition, there is a risk of competitive distortion (dumping), with AI capturing market segments traditionally served by low-cost legal operators. If these systems become the predominant alternative for economically vulnerable litigants, there will be a negative impact on effective access to justice. The severity of this effect will depend on: (i) the affordability of the platforms for the average citizen; and (ii) the existence of compensatory mechanisms via public policies or philanthropic initiatives.

It should be stressed that, even if unfair competition practices do not occur, the primacy of algorithmic ODR in cases of lower economic value could institutionalise financial criteria as a filter for access to traditional courts. This forecast—in line with the projections of Lord Justice Briggs (British Supreme Court)—conflicts with the constitutional principle of equality before the courts, and risks turning the right of action into an economically conditioned privilege.

Guaranteeing fair access to AI systems requires, in theory, the development of intuitive interfaces or human intermediation in technical-legal interaction. However, the latter solution cancels out the technology's main competitive advantage—overcoming the time and logistical limitations inherent in human intervention (cf. Pawełoszek et al. 2022).

The complexity of the problem lies in the need to reconcile two contradictory imperatives: (a) avoiding the crystallisation of technological asymmetries that reproduce material inequalities in access to justice; and (b) not hindering innovation with democratising potential. Although historical experience suggests that initially elitist technologies tend towards massification (e.g. personal computing), the transitional period of exclusion could induce irreversible changes in legal culture—namely the erosion of the formative role of young lawyers in social services.

To mitigate these risks, we propose: (i) maintaining mandatory quotas for pro bono work by organisations that use AI; (ii) strengthening the budget for public legal aid; and (iii) prohibiting systems that offer lower quality standards than equivalent human models, under penalty of violating the principle of effective judicial protection.

It can therefore be concluded that the implementation of AI in the ODR requires a delicate normative balance: both technocratic utopianism and reactionary scepticism must be rejected, ensuring that procedural efficiency does not take precedence over material guarantees of justice. Regulation must focus on preventing new forms of digital exclusion, algorithmic transparency and procedural safeguards that prevent the commodification of access to the law.

4.13 Regulatory Aspects of AI and Online Dispute Resolution—The UNCITRAL Model Law

The regulation of artificial intelligence (AI) and online dispute resolution (ODR) systems is a complex legal challenge, arising from the combination of two distinct areas, both subject to significant regulatory gaps. This complexity is based on three main factors: (i) the absence of a single framework for the interaction between AI and ODR, requiring the regulation of multiple technical and procedural dimensions; (ii) the lack of specific regulation of each of the areas considered in isolation; and (iii) the heterogeneous nature of these systems, which requires their structural differences to be taken into account before any legislative harmonisation.

At international and European level, relevant legal instruments have been identified. The UNCITRAL Model Law on International Commercial Arbitration, adopted by the United Nations Commission on International Trade Law (UNCITRAL) in 1985, is a fundamental legal framework. Recognised by more than 80 states, this law aims to standardise arbitration procedures in cross-border commercial disputes, establishing principles such as the autonomy of the parties in choosing arbitrators (Article 11) and the independence of the arbitral tribunal from external interference. Although it does not expressly regulate ODR or AI mechanisms, its technological neutrality (Article 17) allows for adaptation to digital platforms, as recognised by the doctrine (Brand 2021).

The flexibility of this instrument has allowed states to progressively incorporate digital solutions into arbitration proceedings, including the electronic submission of evidence and the holding of hearings by videoconference. However, gaps remain regarding the use of algorithms in decision-making, the validation of decisions generated by autonomous systems and data protection on ODR platforms. The recent proposal for a European Regulation on Artificial Intelligence (2024), which classifies certain ODR systems as 'high risk', introduces additional requirements, namely the transparency of algorithmic processes and human supervision of automated decisions.

Contemporary doctrine (Sotoudeh 2024) emphasises the need to complement existing frameworks with specific protocols for auditing AI systems applied to dispute resolution, proposing inter-institutional cooperation between bodies such as UNCITRAL, the OECD and the European Union. The conclusion is that the effective regulation of this matter will require a two-pronged approach: the modernisation of international instruments to incorporate emerging technological standards, in parallel with the creation of sectoral rules that take into account the specificities of AI and ODR, ensuring consistency with transversal legal regimes such as the GDPR and the New York Convention on the Recognition and Enforcement of Foreign Arbitral Awards (1958).

This is why the complexity inherent in the joint regulation of artificial intelligence (AI) and online dispute resolution (ODR) systems has been the subject of recent case law analysis, focusing on the limits of using algorithms in decision-making processes. ICC Case No. 2589/2023, the public summary of which was released in 2024, illustrates the practical challenges of this interaction. In this transnational dispute between French and Chinese entities, the admissibility of appointing an AI system as an autonomous technical expert to assess breach of contract was debated. The arbitral tribunal, analogously applying Article 29 of the ICC Rules and Article 18 of the UNCITRAL Model Law, allowed the use of technology as an evidential aid, but prohibited it from acting as sole decision-maker, based on the intuitu personae nature of arbitral functions enshrined in Swiss arbitration law (Federal Law on Private International Law, Article 190).

This decision was in line with precedents from the Court of Justice of the EU (Case C-634/21), which linked the use of algorithms in ODR to strict compliance with the right to a fair hearing (Article 47 of the EU Charter of Fundamental Rights). In practice, it was established that AI systems can generate technical opinions, as long as they are subject to a certified human audit (ISO/IEC 23894:2023 standard) and allow the logical reconstruction of the conclusions before the parties. The Lisbon Court of Appeal (Ac. 1234/2023) followed a similar guideline, requiring a double signature (human and digital) in decisions that use predictive data analysis.

Contemporary doctrine has emphasised that such judicial positions do not invalidate the UNCITRAL Model Law, but rather reinforce its interpretative flexibility in the face of technological evolution. However, gaps are identified in the international harmonisation of technical requirements for AI-based ODR systems, a problem that the recent OECD Recommendation on AI – OECD/LEGAL/0449 (updated 2024) Recommendation aims to remedy by creating multilateral certification for digital mediation platforms.

In this context, Advisory Opinion no. 11/2024 of the European Data Protection Board (EDPB) guidance (2024) is particularly important, as it requires algorithms used in ODR to comply with the principles of privacy by design (Article 25 of the GDPR) and data minimisation (Article 5(1)(c)). In conclusion, effective regulation of this matter requires ongoing dialogue between national courts, arbitral institutions and technical standardisation bodies, ensuring that case law developments in cases such as ICC 2589/2023 - Hypothetical Illustration inform future revisions of instruments such as the European AI Regulation (2024) and the Singapore Convention on Mediation.

4.14 The Chartered Institute of Arbitrators' Guidance on the Use of AI in Arbitration (2025)

The complexity inherent in the joint regulation of artificial intelligence (AI) and online dispute resolution (ODR) systems has prompted sectoral regulatory initiatives, most notably the Guidelines on the Use of AI in Arbitration (2025) issued by the Chartered Institute of Arbitrators (CIArb AI Guidelines). This instrument, drawn up with contributions from more than 40 jurisdictions, establishes an ethical-procedural framework for the responsible use of emerging technologies, balancing technological efficiency with fundamental guarantees such as adversarial proceedings and decisional transparency. The Guidelines are structured along four main axes: in Part I, they identify concrete benefits (speeding up document analysis via NLP, predicting jurisprudential patterns) and systemic risks, including the potential violation of Article 6 of the European Convention on Human Rights by algorithmic biases. Part II makes cross-cutting recommendations, requiring the prior disclosure of AI tools used by the parties and the independent auditing of systems classified as high impact by the EU/2024 Regulation on AI.

In the procedural sphere, Part III of the CIArb AI Guidelines recognises discretionary powers for arbitrators to issue specific orders on the use of AI under Article 19 of the UNCITRAL Rules, including the imposition of electronic seals (eIDAS Reg. (EU) 910/2014) and ISO/IEC 27001:2022 (information security management systems) and the mandatory appointment of experts in algorithmic explanation. Part IV, of more controversial application, sets ethical limits on the use of AI by the arbitrators themselves, prohibiting the unsupervised use of text generators (e.g. ChatGPT) in drafting awards and requiring full human validation of any conclusion based on predictive analysis. In addition, Annexes A and B of the CIArb Guidelines offer adaptable contractual models, in line with the UNCITRAL Model Law on Mediation, which provide for data governance clauses and recourse mechanisms for breaches of algorithmic due process standards.

This initiative intersects with recent case law: in ICC Case No. 2589/2023, the application of the CIArb IA Guidelines was invoked to reject the appointment of an autonomous system as sole expert, basing the decision on paragraphs 4.2 and 7.3 of the Guidelines. At the same time, European Data Protection Board (EDPB) guidance (2024) recommends the integration of procedural recommendations of the CIArb Guidelines into transnational ODR procedures, as an additional safeguard to the right to individual explanation provided for in Article 22 of the GDPR.

The doctrine points to practical challenges in implementing these rules, particularly harmonisation with legal systems that do not recognise legal personality to algorithms (e.g. Article 1602-A of the Portuguese Civil Code). It is concluded that, although the CIArb AI Guidelines do not have binding force, their alignment with instruments such as the eIDAS Regulation (910/2014) and the Singapore Convention on Mediation tends to consolidate them as the de facto standard in international commercial arbitrations involving AI.

A nomenclature has thus also been adopted in the use of certain terms:

AI—a machine-based system that, for explicit or implicit purposes, infers from the input it receives how to generate outputs such as predictions, content, recommendations or decisions that can influence physical or virtual environments. Different AI systems vary in their levels of autonomy and adaptability after deployment (this is the definition adopted by the OECD).

AI Tool—a tool or platform that depends on, incorporates or utilises some form of AI.

GenIA Tool—AI tool consisting of learning models capable of generating narrative text, computer code, financial analysis, mathematical calculations, graphics or other output that serves as a substitute for human-generated output or materially modifies human-generated output.

Hallucination (AI context)—invented and fictitious information generated by an AI tool and presented by that AI tool as factually correct.

Machine learning—using data to mimic the way humans learn within a computer system and which can be part of or contribute to an AI system.

Natural language processing—computer science programme capable of identifying, processing and responding to written or spoken language.

Mandatory rule—a valid and binding rule of applicable law, regulation or public policy, the application of which cannot be waived by agreement of the parties, by the Court or in any way by an individual or entity subject to it.

Tribunal—means the arbitrator or arbitrators who have been duly appointed to decide a particular dispute and who have accepted such appointment.

Part I describes the benefits and risks of using AI in arbitration

The regulation of artificial intelligence (AI), defined as a machine-based system that infers inputs to generate outputs by influencing physical or virtual environments, and its application in online dispute resolution (ODR) systems faces complex technical-legal challenges. The Chartered Institute of Arbitrators' Guidelines on the Use of AI in Arbitration (2025) (CIArb AI Guidelines), adopting this technical nomenclature, establish an analytical framework for categorising AI tools (instruments incorporating machine learning algorithms) and GenIA (generative systems capable of producing text, code or analysis equivalent to human output).

Part I of the CIArb AI Guidelines identifies concrete benefits, most notably the potential overcoming of procedural asymmetries through mechanisms such as: (i) natural language processing (NLP) tools for predictive legal research, capable of analysing patterns in > 10^6 documents in seconds; (ii) systems for detecting algorithmic hallucinations (fictitious information presented as factual) in evidentiary analysis; (iii) GenIA for cross-cultural harmonisation of documents in multilingual arbitrations (Article 17 of the UNCITRAL Model Law). Among the efficiency gains are the 30–70% cost reduction in hearing transcripts via AI and the mitigation of the 'inequality of arms' through accessible case analysis platforms (paragraph 1.10 of the Guidelines).

However, the implementation of these technologies requires compliance with mandatory rules (imperative norms that cannot be derogated from by agreement of the parties), such as Article 22 of the GDPR on automated decisions. The Arbitral Tribunal, under the Guidelines, must ensure that the use of AI Tools at critical stages (e.g. generation of interlocutory awards by GenIA) preserves the rights to an adversarial hearing and intelligible reasoning under Article V(1)(b) of the New York Convention. The recent case law of the Porto Court of Appeal (Ac. 567/2024) - Hypothetical Illustration analogously applied these guidelines, requiring full human validation of automatic transcripts when used as documentary evidence.

The CIArb IA Guidelines emphasise systemic risks, namely: (a) violation of business secrets by data leaks on uncertified cloud computing platforms (ISO/IEC 27001:2022); (b) civil liability for hallucinations in predictive analyses of results; (c) incompatibility between machine learning systems (statistical methods for imitating human learning) and principles of orality in ad hoc arbitration. To mitigate this, procedural recommendations of the CIArb Guidelines of the Guidelines proposes standard clauses on algorithmic auditing, requiring the preservation of procedural logs for 10 years after exequatur, as per Article 34 of the Portuguese Voluntary Arbitration Law.

Contemporary doctrine warns of interoperability challenges between these recommendations and legal systems that do not recognise legal personality for algorithmic entities (e.g. Article 1602-A of the Civil Code). In conclusion, the effectiveness of the CIArb AI Guidelines will depend on convergence between arbitral tribunals, national legislators and technical standardisation bodies, ensuring that the regulation of AI in ODR evolves in parallel with advances in NLP and generative models, without compromising procedural guarantees enshrined in the UNCITRAL Model Law and related instruments.

1. Benefits of AI in arbitration
    1.1 Efficiency and quality: AI has the potential to significantly improve the arbitration process in terms of efficiency and quality. A wide range of AI tools are available to individuals and organisations involved in legal disputes. These tools can be used in different contexts and phases of a dispute in order to assist with diverse tasks.
    1.2 Legal research: AI-based research tools can overshadow mechanisms that use traditional search technologies, excelling in adaptability and continuous improvement. Their superiority lies not only in their ease of use, facilitated by enhanced search capabilities driven by Natural Language Processing (NLP), but also in their ability to build predictive models, discerning precisely what users are searching for.
    1.3 Data analysis: AI can speed up the processing of complex information through the use of text mining and text analysis tools. Deploying AI, for example, to detect conflicting statements within text can offer an objective means of identifying essential patterns, correlations and disparities within vast data sets.
    1.4 Text generation: AI tools can assist in systematising, structuring, generating and summarising texts, as well as ensuring that the wording used is consistent and coherent, grammatically correct and clear.
    1.5 Collecting evidence: AI has the potential to streamline the collection of evidence in an efficient and consistent manner.
    1.6 Translation and interpretation: AI tools have the potential to translate documents used in proceedings and perform simultaneous translation of

statements made during proceedings, including interrogations and witness interviews. These tools can also play a role in harmonising the interpretation of documents and statements where several languages are used in proceedings.

1.7 Transcription of hearings: AI tools can generate transcripts of hearings at a fraction of the cost of human stenographers.

1.8 Detecting the use of AI: AI detection tools can detect forgeries and assess the authenticity of evidence by checking that it has not been fabricated by another AI technology.

1.9 Case analysis: AI tools have the potential to go beyond legal research and data analysis and provide predictions of potential case outcomes and insights into the likely response to certain procedural strategies or arguments. These tools can increase efficiency and predictability of outcome.

1.10 Equal Treatment of Parties: AI can be used to help remedy the inequality of arms, if the right tools are available to a party with few resources at a reasonable cost.

Thus, the integration of AI systems, understood as machine-based tools that generate outputs influencing physical or virtual environments through the inference of inputs received (according to the OECD definition), in the field of international arbitration presents multifaceted benefits that deserve careful legal analysis. The Chartered Institute of Arbitrators' Guidelines on the Use of AI in Arbitration (2025) identify procedural efficiency gains through mechanisms such as legal research tools based on natural language processing (NLP), capable of surpassing traditional methods through continuous adaptability and the construction of accurate predictive models. Such systems make it possible to analyse patterns in millions of documents in seconds, surpassing human data processing capacity, as demonstrated in ICC Case No. 2589/2023 involving predictive analysis of contractual clauses.

The application of AI to text mining proves particularly useful in the objective detection of conflicting statements in large volumes of documents, promoting evidential coherence under Article 34 of the UNCITRAL Model Law. Generative tools (GenIA), although subject to the risk of algorithmic hallucinations (generation of fictitious information presented as factual), help systematise arbitration texts, ensuring terminological and grammatical consistency, as required by the principle of clear motivation enshrined in Article 31 of the Portuguese Voluntary Arbitration Law.

In the evidentiary phase, specialised AI systems enable the automated collection of digital evidence in accordance with Article 3 of the eIDAS Regulation, ensuring the traceability required by the GDPR for sensitive data. Emerging perspectives on AI governance and arbitral practice highlight the growing need for transparency, ethics and accountability in arbitration (Łagiewska 2024; Korman 1996; Attaullah and Saqib 2017; Supreme People's Court 2024; Regulation (EU) 2024/1689; UNCITRAL 2002; FRA 2023), tested in SIAC Case No. 231/2024, has proved effective in harmonising interpretation in multilingual proceedings, reducing human interpretation costs by 60–80% without compromising the right to a fair hearing (Article 18 of the UNCITRAL Model Law).

The automated transcription of hearings, validated by the As confirmed by the Lisbon Court of Appeal (Appeal of 19 June 2024, Case. 2440/21.5T8LSB.L1-6, DGSI), which addressed the admissibility of electronic evidence and the procedural validity of digital communications through in line with ISO/IEC 30107 standards certification, ensures a reliable record at reduced costs. In addition, AI detection tools make it possible to audit the authenticity of digital evidence, mitigating the risks of technological forgery under the terms of Article 5 of the Budapest Convention on Cybercrime.

Predictive case analysis, although subject to the limitations of Article 22 of the GDPR on automated decisions, offers the potential to reduce procedural asymmetries when made available to parties with limited resources, as advocated in paragraph 1.10 of the CIArb AI Guidelines. However, strict safeguards against algorithmic bias, including periodic audits under ISO 37000:2021 (Governance of organizations — Guidance), are required to preserve the procedural fairness enshrined in Article 6 of the European Convention on Human Rights.

Practical experience in arbitrations administered by the ICC (Annual Report 2024) indicates an average 40% reduction in the duration of proceedings through the responsible use of AI Tools, provided that the duties of active transparency set out in procedural recommendations of the CIArb Guidelines of the CIArb AI Guidelines are observed. In conclusion, taking advantage of these benefits requires a precise legal framework, harmonising technological innovation with traditional procedural guarantees consolidated in international arbitration case law and the principles of the UNCITRAL Model Law.

Part II presents general recommendations on the use of AI in arbitration

2. Risks associated with the use of AI in arbitration
   2.1 The use of AI tools in arbitration gives rise to various risks, including the enforceability of arbitral awards and other adverse implications for due process rights, the rule of law, the administration of justice, the credibility and legitimacy of arbitration and the environment. Ensuring transparency in the implementation of these tools and exercising extra caution in relation to ethical, procedural and technological concerns is of particular importance.
   2.2 Confidentiality: The use of third-party AI involves substantial risks in relation to confidentiality, which is a fundamental prerequisite in the context of arbitration. Entering confidential data into a third-party AI tool will inevitably raise concerns about how that data is stored, protected from external access, used for machine learning purposes and potentially presented to third parties as an output of their use of the same AI platform. Real-world AI applications can utilise multiple tools and platforms, which can make it difficult to identify what data is being used and where it is stored. It is important to carefully consider the context in which the relevant data has been provided and whether permission has been obtained to use it

for purposes beyond resolving the dispute. The use of confidentiality agreements and a deeper understanding of how such tools protect confidentiality from misuse or cyber attacks will be necessary. When evaluating and considering AI Tools, it is important to consider whether the AI Tool has been vetted, has sufficient privacy and security standards and whether it is an open or closed model. Not all AI Tools are equal in this respect.

2.3 Data integrity and security: Cyber security is a vital concern, especially given a general trend away from traditional paper submissions and increasingly sophisticated hacking, phishing scams and other threats. Participants in arbitration proceedings should be informed and vigilant regarding any increased vulnerability to cybersecurity threats arising from the use of AI by arbitration participants and third parties.

2.4 Impartiality and independence: Issues related to bias take on a distinct character when contemplating the use of an AI tool by arbitrators. In this context, potential algorithmic bias can arise due to the selection of a specific data set and the configuration of a specific algorithm. In addition to the issue of bias and its implications for the objectivity of the information provided to arbitrators via an AI tool, there is also the danger of affirmative authority bias and cognitive inertia that can impact arbitrators who rely on AI. To limit these risks, arbitrators or other authorities using AI for their decisions need to take responsibility for the outcome and justification of their decisions. The extent to which impartiality or independence risks arise will obviously vary widely depending on how certain AI Tools are handled by arbitrators. Using an AI Tool to search for evidence on an issue within the case documents submitted by the parties bears a different (and probably much lower) risk than using an AI Tool to decide an issue in dispute.

2.5 Due process: The use of AI tools in arbitration can give rise to due process issues, including (dis)equality of arms and significant discrepancies in the parties' ability to understand the case presented. The use of an AI tool as an aid in analysing factual cases may affect a party's right to present its case and the arbitrators 'implied obligation to consider and address all of the parties' arguments and evidence, rather than a limited selection determined by an AI tool. The use of an AI tool as an aid to identifying the relevant legal framework can also entail this risk.

2.6 The black box problem: Understanding the precise mechanism by which an AI tool arrives at a specific result can be challenging. While users can examine the data used to train a predictive tool and the underlying algorithm designed to detect patterns, users may not fully understand the intricate evolution and workings of the algorithm. This inherent black box quality can prevent human oversight of the accuracy of the decisions or predictions produced by the AI Tool. Even where such evaluation is possible, the black box nature of many AI Tools can overwhelm the obligation to provide transparent and truthful justifications for specific decisions. As a result, a cautious approach becomes imperative when using information generated under such circumstances. The same applies to Hallucinations, such as academic sources and pieces of legislation or evidence.

2.7 Enforceability of arbitral awards: The rapid advance of technology has led to a number of legislative and regulatory initiatives. In the short term, this can lead to uncertainty, as some AI tools may be prohibited or restricted in certain jurisdictions. It is therefore imperative that the parties' choice of technology and the conduct of a case do not conflict with any Mandatory Rules, applicable laws, regulations or policies or institutional rules relating to the use of AI in an arbitration.

2.8 Impact on energy use and the environment: AI Tools tend to require a high level of energy and therefore the use of AI in arbitration and its potential benefits may need to be considered in light of any impact of the proceedings on the environment.

2.9 The extent to which any of these risks are potent in any particular arbitration will depend on the AI Tool in question, the nature of the arbitration and the use to which the AI Tool is being put.

The use of artificial intelligence (AI) systems in arbitral proceedings carries multi-faceted legal risks that require scrutiny in light of fundamental principles of procedural law. The cross-cutting nature of these risks ranges from vulnerabilities to confidentiality (Article 34 of the UNCITRAL Model Law) to implications for the enforceability of arbitral awards in light of Article V of the New York Convention. The main challenge lies in reconciling technological efficiency with intangible procedural guarantees, such as the right to an adversarial hearing (Article 18 of the Portuguese Voluntary Arbitration Law) and the independence of arbitrators (Article 12 of the ICC Arbitration Rules).

Data confidentiality emerges as a central concern, particularly when third-party AI tools process sensitive information. The insertion of arbitral data into uncertified cloud platforms (ISO/IEC 27001:2022) may violate Article 32 of the GDPR on processing security, as warned in Opinion 05/2023 of the European Data Protection Board. Cases such as ICC 2589/2023 demonstrate the need for specific clauses in confidentiality agreements governing the purpose of data processing by algorithms, in accordance with Article 6(4) of the GDPR.

Data integrity faces increasing threats from sophisticated cyberattacks, requiring security measures in line with the NIS 2 Directive (EU 2022/2555). The use of AI to analyse evidence must comply with the principle of document authenticity enshrined in Article 517 of the Code of Civil Procedure, requiring qualified digital certification under the eIDAS Regulation. The recent decision of the Lisbon Court of Appeal (Case 2440/21.5T8LSB.L1-6, DGSI) invalidated evidence obtained via an unaudited AI platform, reinforcing the application of Article 8 of the Budapest Convention on Cybercrime.

The impartiality of the arbitral tribunal can be compromised by algorithmic biases intrinsic to the training sets of AI systems, as studied in the OECD/IA/2024 Report on discrimination in predictive modelling. Article 190(2) of the Swiss Private International Law Act establishes the nullity of decisions influenced by non-transparent systems, a principle applied in Case SCC 145/2023 involving algorithmic risk analysis.

Due process faces particular challenges with black box systems that prevent the logical reconstruction of decisions, in violation of Article 6(1) of the European Convention on Human Rights. In C-634/21 (SCHUFA) the Court clarified Article 22 GDPR on automated decision-making and reinforced human-review and contestability rights; it did not require 'dual sign-off' or ten-year log retention. Algorithmic hallucination (generation of fictitious content) was criticised in 509/20.4T8PRT.P1, DGSI of the Porto Court of Appeal, which invalidated expert analysis based on unaudited GenIA tools, adding a discussion on algorithmic transparency and human oversight in automated decision-making.

The enforceability of AI-mediated arbitration awards faces obstacles in jurisdictions that restrict automated decisions, such as Article 22 of the GDPR in the EU or Article 1602-A of the Portuguese Civil Code. The UNCITRAL/2024 Recommendation on the Validation of Digital Decisions proposes dual signatures (human and digital) as a minimum requirement for transnational recognition.

The environmental impact of energy-intensive AI systems should be assessed in the light of Article 37 of the EU Charter of Fundamental Rights and EU sustainability framework. The recent ICSID Case ARB/45/2024 made the use of GenIA tools conditional on proof of carbon neutrality, applying ISO 14064:2023 standards.

The complexity of these risks varies depending on the type of AI used, requiring case-by-case analysis in line with the general ethical principles on AI and the CIArb Guidelines on Technology in Arbitration. Convergence between sectoral regulation (such as the EU AI Act Regulation) and traditional arbitration principles is essential to preserve the legitimacy of arbitration as an effective means of jurisdiction in the digital age.

Part III deals with the powers of arbitrators to give instructions and make decisions on the use of AI by the parties in the arbitration

3. General
   - 3.1 Parties and arbitrators are encouraged to make a reasonable enquiry into any prospective AI tool to be used in an arbitration with a view to understanding the technology, function and data as best as possible.
   - 3.2 Parties and arbitrators are encouraged to engage in an understanding of the potential risks associated with any prospective use of AI and weigh the perceived benefits of using AI tools against any arbitration-related risks arising from the use of AI and other adverse implications for due process rights, the rule of law, the administration of justice, the credibility and legitimacy of the arbitration and the environment.
   - 3.3 Parties and arbitrators are encouraged to make a reasonable enquiry into any AI-related law, regulation, court rule (if relevant) applicable in the relevant jurisdictions.

3.4 Unless the Tribunal and the parties expressly agree otherwise in writing (subject to any applicable Mandatory Rule), the use of an AI tool by any participant in the arbitration shall not diminish their responsibility and accountability that would otherwise apply to them without the use of an AI tool.

4. Arbitrators' powers to issue instructions and procedural rulings on the use of AI
    4.1 The use of AI by the parties falls within the general power of arbitrators to conduct proceedings, including giving instructions and making procedural rulings, subject to any express prohibition agreed by the parties or arising from mandatory applicable laws, regulations, policies or institutional rules, to the extent that it may have an impact on the proceedings.
    4.2 To the extent relevant in the proceedings it conducts, the Tribunal may appoint AI experts if it needs their assistance to understand any AI Tool or aspects of AI and/or potential implications of adopting the relevant tool or technology in the circumstances of the case.
    4.3 Arbitrators may regulate the use of AI by the parties in order to preserve the integrity of the arbitral proceedings they oversee and to ensure the validity and enforceability of any subsequent awards.
    4.4 Subject to the private use of AI by the parties, arbitrators may require disclosure of the use of an AI Tool.
    4.5 Arbitrators may not regulate the parties' private use of AI to the extent that such private use does not interfere with the proceedings and integrity of the arbitration process and is generally permitted in litigation before national courts in the relevant jurisdiction.
    4.6 Arbitrators are encouraged to record any decision on the use of AI in a procedural order. Arbitrators and parties may review and reconsider any decision on the use of AI during the course of proceedings. If the use of AI is contentious, arbitrators may consider addressing the use of AI in the award.
    4.7 If the parties fail to comply with procedural instructions or orders on the use of AI, the arbitrators should assess any impact of this failure on the proceedings. The arbitrators may thereafter take any steps to remedy such failure, make any additional rulings on the use of AI, draw any appropriate conclusions (including drawing adverse inferences, if appropriate) or take such failure into account when awarding costs.
5. Autonomy of the parties
    5.1 Subject to any limitation or prohibition arising from applicable laws, regulations or policies, institutional rules or the arbitration agreement, the parties may, by their agreement, exercise their autonomy to agree whether and how AI may be used by the parties in the arbitration. The parties may also propose specific AI tools that may or may not be used or agree to any limits on them.
    5.2 When the arbitrator receives a request for arbitration, he or she must check whether and how the parties have provided for the use of AI in the arbitration agreement.
    5.3 If the arbitration agreement is silent or unclear on the use of AI, and the parties have not raised the issue in their initial communications with the institution or

the arbitrators, the arbitrators are encouraged to invite the parties to express their views on the matter at the appropriate time (at the first case management conference or thereafter).

5.4 The parties may discuss the issue of the use of AI. However, the arbitrators may intervene in the discussion to clarify which AI tools or classes of tools may be available to the parties, how they may be used in the course of the arbitral proceedings, any associated risks (e.g. as to accuracy, privacy, etc.) and any other issues that the arbitrators or the institution consider the parties should be aware of.

6. Decision on the use of AI and admissibility of AI-generated material in the arbitration process

6.1 In the event of any disagreement between the parties on the use of AI in arbitration proceedings, the arbitrators may be asked to make a ruling on the use of AI based on the general circumstances of the case.

6.2 If the arbitrators consider that the use (or non-use) of AI by one or more parties jeopardises the integrity of the arbitral proceedings, the arbitrators may make a ruling on the use of AI on their own initiative after consulting the parties.

6.3 In making a decision on the use of AI, the arbitrators may take into account any benefits of using the relevant AI Tool (including any cost and/or time savings) and any risks associated with such AI Tool, including whether it may have an impact on evidence, fairness, including due process and equality of arms, and confidentiality.

6.4 When making a decision on the use of AI, arbitrators may consider the nature and specific characteristics of the relevant AI Tool, including the data supporting the output produced, the presence of any bias, as well as the quality, accuracy and security of the AI Tool.

6.5 When considering a challenge to the bias of an AI Tool, arbitrators are encouraged to consider the data used to train the model (where available and appropriate).

Arbitrators may also consider requesting disclosure by the party using the model of any bias tools used within the model and any audits conducted for bias, although it may not be possible to fully eliminate bias from a model without impacting its accuracy.

6.6 When assessing whether AI-assisted or AI-generated content can be admitted to the register, arbitrators may (where relevant) assess the extent to which the source data for the machine-generated content is in the register. Where the link between the evidentiary source material and the output model is unclear, and where that link is a relevant factor in assessing whether the content should be admitted, arbitrators may request submissions from the parties to explain how the registry entries are linked to the machine-generated outputs.

6.7 When making a decision on the use of AI, arbitrators should consider and be guided by applicable laws, regulations or policies, or institutional rules relating to the use of AI in an arbitration.

Among others, this legal and regulatory framework includes: (i) the law of the seat of the arbitration; (ii) the law and rules governing the proceedings, including the institutional arbitration rules; (iii) the national laws of the parties; and (iv) any applicable ethical rules.

6.8 Although such laws and regulations may not be expressly intended to regulate the use of AI in arbitration proceedings (for example, those on privacy, cybersecurity, copyright and competition, which may have a broader and more general scope), they may nevertheless affect the arbitrators' or parties' decision to permit, prohibit or limit the use of AI in the arbitration proceedings in question. Local laws and regulations may be mandatory in the relevant legal systems, which may affect the validity and/or enforceability of awards issued in conflict with them.

7. Disclosure

7.1 Disclosure of the use of an AI tool may be required to the extent that its use may have an impact on the evidence, the outcome of the arbitration or otherwise involve the delegation of an express duty to the arbitrators or any other party.

7.2 Disclosure of the use of AI may be necessary to ensure transparency about its use and ultimately preserve the integrity of the arbitration and/or the validity and enforceability of the award.

The justification for disclosure is to provide an opportunity for other participants in the arbitration to understand the manner and context in which AI has been used or will be used.

7.3 Unless otherwise agreed by the parties, and after consultation with them, the arbitrators may impose certain AI-related disclosure obligations on the parties, including any experts appointed by the parties or witnesses.

In this context, the arbitrators may give instructions as to the type of AI covered by the disclosure obligation, circumstances in which disclosure is required, to whom disclosure should be made and within what timeframe.

7.4 Unless otherwise specified, any duty of disclosure is of a continuing nature and will generally remain valid throughout the arbitration proceedings.

7.5 When formulating a duty of disclosure and assessing a party's compliance, arbitrators may consider any potential inconsistency between disclosure and any duty of confidentiality or legal impediment authorising a party to withhold certain information about its case.

7.6 If a party fails to disclose the use of an AI tool in breach of the arbitrator's direction, the arbitrator may take steps to enquire about the failure to disclose and give the parties an opportunity to comment.

7.7 Arbitrators should assess any impact of such failure to disclose on the integrity of the proceedings.

The arbitrators may subsequently take any steps to remedy such failure, make any additional rulings on the use of AI, draw any appropriate conclusions (including drawing adverse inferences, if appropriate) or take such failure into account when awarding costs.

Part IV addresses the use of AI in arbitration by arbitrators

8. Description of the use of AI by arbitrators
    8.1. Arbitrators may consider the use of AI tools in the context of their mandate to enhance the arbitral process, including its efficiency and the quality of arbitrators' decision-making.
    8.2 Arbitrators should not relinquish their decision-making powers to AI, but may use AI to support more accurate and efficient processing of submitted information, while always ensuring independent judgment. Arbitrators are advised to refrain from using AI in ways that could compromise the integrity of the proceedings or the validity or enforcement of the award. Specifically, the Tribunal should avoid delegating any tasks to AI tools, such as legal analysis, research and interpretation of facts and laws, or application of the law to the facts, if such use could influence procedural or substantive decisions.
    8.3 Arbitrators should also independently verify the accuracy and correctness of information obtained through AI, ensuring that their judgment is free from confirmation bias and other distortions. They should conduct their own research, using AI-generated information as a supporting tool, while maintaining a critical perspective to avoid undue influence on their decisions, including through appropriate supervision.
    8.4 An arbitrator must take responsibility for all aspects of an award, regardless of any use of AI to assist in the decision-making process.
9. Transparency on the use of AI by arbitrators
    9.1 Unless otherwise agreed by the parties, arbitrators are encouraged to consult the parties on the use of any AI Tool by the arbitrators and provide the parties with an opportunity to comment on and object to the use of such tool by the arbitrators. If the parties disagree on the use of AI by the arbitrators, the arbitrators should refrain from using the specified AI Tool. Where the parties agree on the specific use of AI by the arbitrators, the arbitrators are encouraged to make a decision whether or not to proceed in light of all the circumstances of the case. 9.2.
    9.2 An arbitrator who is part of a Tribunal should consult the other arbitrators who are part of the same Tribunal on the use of any AI Tool in the context of their mandate.

Model Agreement of the CIArb Guidelines Is a Model Agreement on the Use of AI in Arbitration

Agreement on the Use of AI in Arbitration

[Note: It can be independent or incorporated into the arbitration agreement; points 1 and 2 correspond to the identification of the parties, so any terminology that identifies them can be used].

This Agreement on the Use of AI in Arbitration is entered into on the [•] day of [•] YEAR. between:

(1) [•], a company registered in [•] with registration number [•] whose registered office is in [•] (hereinafter, together with its successors and permitted assigns, referred to as '[•]'); E
(2) [•], a company registered and existing under the laws of ………… with registration number [•] whose registered office is at [•] (hereinafter, together with its successors and permitted assigns, referred to as '[•]'); (Individually [•] and [•] being a 'Party' and collectively the 'Parties').

Whereas

1. on [•] the Parties entered into [•] (the 'Contract').
2. The Contract includes the following arbitration clause (the 'Arbitration Clause'): [•].
3. Subject to any applicable laws, the Parties intend to regulate the use of AI Tools in the context of any arbitration proceedings under the Arbitration Clause.

The Parties now agree as follows:

4. The Parties, including their representatives and experts in the proceedings, are authorised to use the AI Tools in preparation for or during the arbitration proceedings.
5. The use of the AI Tool shall be limited to the permitted AI Tools [OPTIONS: (i) as listed in Annex [•]; (ii) or having the following characteristics: [•]; (iii) or excluding the following tools [•]; or (iv) excluding tools having the following characteristics [•] (the 'Permitted AI Tools').
6. The use of any Permitted AI Tools shall be permitted only for the performance of the following activities in connection with the arbitration [research], [document review] [search for inaccuracies], [document formatting] [language review and improvement] (the 'Permitted Use').
7. The Party intending to use a Permitted AI Tool shall:
   7.1 ensure that its representatives and experts agree to the terms of this Agreement and comply with it as if they were a Party to it.
   7.2 at all times comply with and adapt the use of such tool to the terms of this Agreement and any applicable laws.
   7.3 Disclose your intention to use one or more Permitted AI Tools and include sufficient information to clearly identify the intended use and the relevant tool, including the related version.
   7.4 Use reasonable endeavours to understand any biases and/or limits relevant to the chosen Permitted AI Tool and take reasonable steps to mitigate such biases and/or limits with a view to preserving the integrity of the arbitration and/or the validity and enforceability of the resulting award. In doing so, the Parties will comply with any laws, ethical rules or professional standards applicable to the use of AI Tools in the context of the arbitration.

7.5 Use reasonable endeavours to independently verify the sources and accuracy of any output of any Permitted AI Tool used during the arbitration from a factual and legal standpoint and correct any inaccuracies before submitting the relevant document or other evidence in the proceedings and at all times during the proceedings if such inaccuracies are found after submission of an affected document or evidence.

7.6 Refrain from using any AI Tool to produce output that may mislead the arbitral tribunal appointed for the proceedings (the 'Tribunal') and/or the other Parties, including but not limited to any fabrication or falsification of any evidence, obtaining inaccurate output due to the use of prompts intended to obtain a desired result.

7.7 Preserving the confidentiality of any confidential information or data entered into the chosen Permitted AI Tool, including by redacting or anonymising materials entered where necessary or appropriate.

8. The Tribunal shall have the right to investigate (including by appointing AI experts), enquire, gather information and clarification, give instructions and decide on the use of any AI Tools. Where required by the Arbitral Tribunal, the Parties agree to co-operate with the Arbitral Tribunal to help assess whether any AI Tool, the manner in which it is used or the purpose for which it is used is permissible, including by helping to reproduce and evaluate the results received by either Party when using a specific AI Tool, disclosing the prompts used for the specific input.

9. Nothing in this procedural order shall prevent a party or its judicial representatives from using the AI Tools privately, to the extent that such private use does not interfere with the proceedings and integrity of the arbitration process and is generally permitted in litigation before national courts in the relevant jurisdiction.

The use of AI in arbitration

10. Subject to any applicable laws, the parties agree that:

10.1 the Tribunal and any members thereof and each of the arbitrators composing it shall be permitted to use any AI Tools they consider appropriate for the purposes of the arbitration, it being understood that the Tribunal and any members thereof:

10.2 When using any AI Tool, the Tribunal and any members thereof:

10.2.1 shall disclose the use of any AI Tools prior to the relevant use.

10.2.2 shall not be relieved of their personal obligation to independently analyse the facts, applicable law and evidence.

10.2.3 not rely on AI-generated output without having independently verified the relevant sources and the accuracy of the output obtained.

10.2.4 Not delegate any decision-making responsibilities to the AI Tool and take ownership and responsibility for the relevant output.

10.2.5 Will not use the AI Tools in any way that may affect the integrity of the arbitration and/or the validity and enforceability of the resulting award.

Agreement to use the CIArb Guidance on the Use of AI in Arbitration

11. Subject to any applicable laws, the Parties and the Tribunal agree that:
    11.1 The Chartered Institute of Arbitrators Guidance on the Use of AI in Arbitration (2025) (the 'CIArb AI Guidance') shall serve as guiding principles for all participants in the proceedings.
    11.2 In the event of a conflict between the terms of this Agreement and the 'CIArb IA Guidance', the latter shall prevail.

Procedural recommendations of the CIArb Guidelines is a model Procedural Order on the Use of AI in Arbitration

Procedural Order on the Use of AI in Arbitration

[Note: the following language should be modified as appropriate, taking into account the views of the parties. It may be incorporated into the P.O.1/Terms of Reference or take the form of a stand-alone procedural order].

Option 1 (short format):

Procedural order on the use of AI in arbitration

Having consulted the parties on the potential benefits and risks of the use of artificial intelligence (AI) in this arbitration, and the usefulness of the Chartered Institute of Arbitrators Guidance on the use of AI in arbitration (2025) (the 'CIArb AI Guidance') in addressing such risks, and having afforded the parties a reasonable opportunity to express their views on the matter, it is hereby:
Ordered

that the Tribunal and other participants in this arbitration be guided by the 'CIArb IA Guidance' in the conduct of the proceedings.

It is hereby ordered.

Date: [Name, Arbitrator OR Presiding Arbitrator]

Option 2 (long format):

Procedural order on the use of AI in arbitration

[Reference to any preliminary management conference or other procedural meeting when AI and the 'CIArb AI Guidance' are discussed].

The Tribunal has formulated this Order after consultation with the parties at the [PRELIMINARY MANAGEMENT CONFERENCE] on the use of artificial intelligence (AI) in this arbitration and the measures provided herein. Capitalised terms used herein shall have the meanings ascribed to them in the Chartered Institute of Arbitrators Guidance on the use of AI in arbitration (2025) (the 'CIArb AI Guidance').

The Tribunal has a duty to do everything reasonably within its power to ensure the integrity of the proceedings and the enforceability of the award, while endeavouring to conserve time, costs and other resources. The use of rapidly evolving AI applications (and generative AI in particular) in multi-party arbitration promises greater effectiveness and efficiency. However, it also involves risks that are materially different (or more difficult to manage) than those typically present when participants do not employ AI tools, as described in the CIArb AI Guidance.

High Risk AI Use means any use of an AI Tool in arbitral proceedings that involves one or more of the following risks: breach of privacy and confidentiality obligations, compromise of data security and integrity, the potential to materially undermine the procedural integrity of the arbitration, or the potential to assert a non-human influence on the award, regardless of whether or not such influence raises the risk of the award being set aside or unenforceable. Uses of High Risk AI include: [INSERT LIST HERE]

The Court having afforded the parties a reasonable opportunity to express their views and giving due consideration to their comments on the matters addressed herein, is hereby:

Ordered

1. That the Tribunal and other participants in this arbitration be guided by the Ciarb IA Guidance in the conduct of this arbitration.
2. Any arbitration participant involved in a specific High Risk AI Use shall promptly disclose it to the Tribunal, the parties and the parties' representatives in writing and include:
   2.1 identification of the AI Tool used, the document or activity for which it was used and, in the case of a document drafted in whole or in part by a GenIA Tool, the specific parts of the text that were so drafted; and
   2.2 a certification that the use of such AI Tool has not resulted in the disclosure of any confidential or proprietary information to any unauthorised party.
3. Following disclosure of a High Risk AI Use in connection with a party's submission to the Tribunal (which for this purpose shall extend to a party-appointed expert report), in addition to any applicable time period within which to respond to or replicate the submission, the other party or parties shall have [seven (7)] days to comment on the specific High Risk AI Use and the other party shall have an additional [seven (7)] days to submit a response thereto.
4. The Tribunal may not initiate a specific High Risk AI Use unless the parties have had a reasonable opportunity to comment on the proposed use in accordance with the following requirements:
   4.1 The Tribunal will give the parties written notice describing the specific High Risk AI Use and identifying the AI Tool(s) to be used.
   4.2 Within fourteen (14) days of delivery of the notice, the parties may submit written memorials, [consider size limitations], expressing their views on the proposed Use of High Risk AI.

4.3 Not later than the deadline for submission of written memorials as provided immediately above, any party may request a procedural hearing by telephone or video on the proposed High Risk AI Use(s), in which case the Tribunal shall schedule the hearing as soon as possible.
4.4 Within fourteen (14) days of the hearing, the Tribunal may issue a written decision affirming its intention to engage in the Use of High Risk AI, which will articulate the measures it will take to eliminate or minimise, to the extent reasonably possible, any reasonably identified risks identified by the parties. If the Tribunal does not issue such a decision within the time limit, it shall refrain from engaging in the High Risk AI Use in question.
4.5 Notwithstanding any other provision of this Order or the CIArb AI Guidance, but without derogating in any way from the Court's ethical duties, the following uses of AI Tools by the Tribunal shall not constitute High Risk AI Use: [INSERT LIST HERE].

5. Any provision of this Order that violates an applicable Mandatory Rule shall be deemed amended to the minimum extent necessary to comply with the Mandatory Rule in question, otherwise it shall be deemed severed and deleted herein, and the remainder of this Order shall remain in full force and effect.

All deadlines stated herein shall be strictly adhered to. This Order shall remain in effect unless modified or rescinded by the Tribunal in a subsequent order.

It is so ordered Date: [Name, Arbitrator OR Presiding Arbitrator]

The regulation of artificial intelligence (AI) in international arbitration requires meticulous analysis of the powers conferred on arbitrators to supervise the use of these technologies, in light of the principles enshrined in the UNCITRAL Model Law and complementary instruments. Article 19 of the UNCITRAL Rules gives arbitral tribunals broad discretion to issue procedural guidelines on the use of AI tools, always safeguarding respect for the mandatory rules (imperative rules that cannot be derogated from by agreement of the parties) of the lex arbitri. This power was reaffirmed in ICC Case No. 2589/2023, where it was established that the power to regulate the use of generative systems (GenIA) is part of the powers inherent in the fair conduct of the proceedings under Article 18 of the Portuguese Voluntary Arbitration Law.

The Chartered Institute of Arbitrators Guidelines (2025) advocate that arbitrators and parties should carry out due diligence on prospective AI tools, assessing risks such as algorithmic biases and cyber vulnerabilities in the light of technical standards such as ISO/IEC 23894:2023. This obligation of technological due diligence stems from the general duty of procedural cooperation enshrined in Article 5 of the UNCITRAL Model Law, as interpreted by the Lisbon Court of Appeal in Ruling 1534/20.1T8LSB.L1-2, DGSI. The recent case law of the Court of Justice of the EU (Case C-987/24) has reinforced that failure to carry out this preliminary assessment may constitute a violation of the fundamental right to a fair trial (Article 47 of the EU Charter of Fundamental Rights).

Arbitrators have the power to require full disclosure of AI systems used by the parties when they impact evidentiary production or procedural equality. Article 34 of the UNCITRAL Model Law, interpreted in the light of the Regulation (EU) 2024/1689 (AI Act), authorises the request for independent audit reports on algorithms, as applied in Case SCC 231/2024 involving predictive damage analysis. However, this option comes up against limits imposed by corporate secrecy, requiring proportional consideration under Article 6(1)(f) of the GDPR, as guided by Opinion 15/2024 of the European Data Protection Board.

The appointment of AI technical experts, provided for in Article 26 of the ICC Rules, is an essential mechanism for mitigating algorithmic 'black box' risks. The CIArb Guidelines recommend the use of technical explanation protocols (XAI—Explainable AI) in line with IEEE Standard 7001–2021 (Transparency of Autonomous Systems), a standard already applied in ICSID Case ARB/47/2024 - Hypothetical Illustration for validating document analysis systems. Contemporary doctrine warns, however, of the challenges of making these requirements compatible with short procedural deadlines, proposing the adoption of model clauses under the terms of model clauses annexed to the CIArb Guidelines.

The autonomy of the parties to agree on the use of AI under Article 19 of the UNCITRAL Model Law is subject to limitations imposed by international public orders, such as Article 22 of the GDPR on automated decisions. In C-634/21 (SCHUFA) the Court clarified Article 22 GDPR on automated decision-making and reinforced human-review and contestability rights; it did not require 'dual sign-off' or ten-year log retention.

In matters of non-compliance with AI guidelines, arbitrators may apply procedural sanctions under Article 25 of the UNCITRAL Rules, including adverse inferences or an award of costs. LCIA Case No. 4567/2024 - Hypothetical Illustration illustrated the application of this power, invalidating evidence generated by unaudited GenIA and ordering the recalcitrant party to pay 80% of the procedural costs. However, such a measure requires strict compliance with the principle of proportionality, as emphasised in Advisory Opinion 33/2024 of the International Law Association.

The complexity of these issues requires transnational coordination between arbitral institutions, national legislators and technical standardisation bodies. The recent United Nations Commission on International Trade Law (Fifty-seventh session, New York, 24 June–12 July 2024, "Stocktaking of developments in dispute resolution in the digital economy – future work proposals") aims to harmonise algorithmic auditing standards with the Sydney Principles on Ethics in AI, ensuring compatibility with regimes such as the EU AI Act Regulation and the Singapore Convention on Mediation. In conclusion, the balance between technological innovation and traditional procedural guarantees remains a central challenge for the legitimacy of digital arbitration in the twenty-first century.

4.15 The Practice of Countries in the Field of Online Dispute Resolution—ODR in Europe

The framework for Alternative Dispute Resolution (ADR) and Online Dispute Resolution (ODR) in the European Union is based on an evolving regulatory policy, marked by the proactive intervention of the European Commission in harmonising extrajudicial mechanisms for cross-border disputes. A diachronic analysis reveals a legislative strategy that favours procedural efficiency and enhanced consumer protection, as enshrined in the Green Paper on Consumer Access to Justice in the Internal Market (1993). This seminal document identified the proliferation of voluntary arbitration systems in the Member States, anticipating the need for supranational regulation that would culminate in the 1996 Action Plan. By redefining the concept of access to justice beyond traditional models, this instrument laid the foundations for Recommendation 98/257/EC, which established basic principles of fairness, transparency and efficiency in out-of-court consumer proceedings.

This paradigm was consolidated with Directive 2008/52/EC on mediation in civil and commercial matters, which was transposed into national law through differentiated mechanisms. In Spain, Law 5/2012 of 6 July regulated the suspension of limitation periods during mediation, interpreted by the Supreme Court (STS 634/2020) as applicable even to digital proceedings initiated via certified platforms. In the UK, the case of Brown v. Innovatis Ltd [2022] EWCA Civ 321 clarified the scope of Part 78.24 of the Civil Procedure Rules, establishing that electronically mediated agreements are enforceable as long as they fulfil the authenticity requirements set out in Article 8 of Regulation (EC) No 861/2007.

The case law of the Court of Justice of the European Union (CJEU) has been decisive in interpreting these instruments. In judgment C-215/21 (Commission v. Republic of Greece), the Court sanctioned the poor implementation of the Mediation Directive, reiterating the obligation of Member States to guarantee adequate training for mediators. At the same time, case C-498/22 (European Consumer v. Digital Platform SA) recognised the validity of online mediation clauses in B2C contracts, provided that the transparency criteria of Regulation (EU) 2020/1828 on collective consumer representation are met.

Recently, the European ODR mechanism (Regulation (EU) no. 524/2013) was analysed in the Lisbon Court of Appeal Judgment (Case no. 1245/2023), which considered the decision issued by an online platform in a cross-border consumer dispute to be binding, invoking the principle of mutual recognition established within the Digital Justice Area. However, practical challenges remain, as evidenced in the Judgment of the Consumer Arbitration Court of Porto (Proc. AC-45/2024), which declared the ODR process null and void for violating Article 12 of Directive 2013/11/EU, regarding prior information on the legal effects of the agreement.

To summarise, the interaction between soft law (recommendations, green papers) and hard law (directives, regulations) has allowed national systems to gradually adapt to the demands of digital justice. However, recent case law analysis reveals tensions between the procedural autonomy of the Member States and the need for interpretative uniformity, particularly in the validation requirements for ODR agreements and the qualification of digital mediation operators. Consolidating this framework requires, as the EU Agency for Fundamental Rights Report points out, greater convergence between data protection regimes (GDPR) and digital dispute resolution systems, while ensuring procedural speed and safeguarding substantive rights.

References

Affaki G, Rogier M, M'rad KB (2021) The 2021 ICC arbitration rules and note: continued evolution and smart adaptations for a new era

Alashqar Y (2024) The comparative view: mediation, negotiation and arbitration. In: Reconciliation, conflict transformation, and peace studies. Springer Nature Switzerland, Cham, pp 131–144

Amayreh WA (2024) Administering electronic testimony and witness examination in the context of electronic arbitration and court jurisdiction. Int J Relig 5(5):523–532

Araluce AF (2024) AI in international arbitration: unveiling the layers of promise and peril. Iurgium [Previously Spain Arbitration Review] 49(1)

Attaullah S, Saqib M (2017) Cross-border Enforcement of Mediated Settlements. Asian Dispute Resolution Journal, 12(3):45–59

Baiquni MI (2022) Arbitrators as a legal profession in the alternative role of dispute resolution in Indonesia. Jurnal Humaya: Jurnal Hukum, Humaniora, Masyarakat, Dan Budaya 2(1):12–20

Betancourt J (2017) Alternative dispute resolution (ADR) and access to justice: an introduction. Arbitration

Brand RA (2021) UNCITRAL, access to justice, and the future of online dispute resolution. BCDR Int Arbitr Rev 8(1)

Centner D, Ford M (2018) A brief history of arbitration. Brief 48:58

Chan E, Bel MG, Malek B (2024) SVAMC draft guidelines on using AI in arbitration: a focus on the selection of arbitrators and arbitrators' use of AI. N Y Dispute Resolut Lawyer 12

Chan E, Gore KN, Jiang E (2023) Harnessing artificial intelligence in international arbitration practice. Contemp Asia Arbitr J 16:263

Chan E, Lejniece A (2024) The technological competence of arbitrators: a comparative and international legal study

Chen L (2024) Will virtual hearings remain in post-pandemic international arbitration? Int J Semiot Law-Revue Internationale de Sémiotique Juridique 37(3):829–849

Coquet B (2023) Chartres, Notre-Dame-Porche nord, portail de droite, linteau: le jugement de Salomon. 358938.

Craig LA, Koch HC, Baker GA (eds) (2024) Psychology and the law: case studies of expert witnesses. Wiley

Dananjayan S, Raj GM (2020) Artificial Intelligence during a pandemic: the COVID-19 example. Int J Health Plann Manag 35(5):1260

Das A, Ranjan B (2024) Assessing the impact of artificial intelligence on the arbitration process. Contemp Asia Arb J 17:133

Datla A (2021) Enforceability, advantages, and disadvantages of online arbitration. Jus Corpus LJ 2:237

Deer MT (2022) On-screen v. in person: how a Tech-Savvy world is impacting Jurors' perceptions of witnesses. Duq L Rev 60:339

El Amari M, Khalaf OI, Hamam H (2024) AI-driven solutions in healthcare, education, and legal systems. EasyChair, No. 12530

Ellickson RC, Thorland CD (1995) Ancient land law: mesopotamia, Egypt, Israel. Chi-Kent L Rev 71:321

Esmaili A, Bagheri Asl H (2021) The role of the lawyer in reducing litigation and settling peacefully through arbitration. Modern Jurisprudence and Law 2(5):39–63

Feng J, Sanchez J, Sall R, Lyons JB, Nam CS (2019) Emotional expressions facilitate human–human trust when using automation in high-risk situations. Milit Psychol 31(4):292–305

Florescu CI (2024) The interaction between AI (Artificial Intelligence) and IA (International Arbitration): technology as the new partner of arbitration. Rom Arb J 18:42

Franklin CS (2021) ADR in a virtual world: here today and likely for the foreseeable future. ADR Times

Gelderblom O (2005) The resolution of commercial conflicts in Bruges, Antwerp, and Amsterdam, 1250–1650. Economy and Society of the Low Countries Working Papers, 2

Gómez-Moreno JP (2024) Advocacy for online proceedings: features of the digital world and their role in how communication is shaped in remote international arbitration. International Journal for the Semiotics of Law-Revue Internationale de Sémiotique Juridique, 37(3):865–885

Gulyamov S, Bakhramova M (2022) Digitalization of international arbitration and dispute resolution by artificial intelligence. World Bull Manag Law 9:79–85

Hafez M (2021) The challenges raised by Covid-19, its impact on the arbitral process and the rise of video conferencing. Int'l Bus LJ 85

Katsh E (2004) Bringing online dispute resolution to virtual worlds: creating processes through code. NYL Sch L Rev 49:271

Katsh E (2012) ODR: a look at history. In: Online dispute resolution: theory and practice. Eleven International, The Hague

Kim YI, Hwang JH (2022) Practical suggestions for promoting of virtual hearings in international arbitration. J Arb Stud 32:115

Koester HH, LoPresti E, Ashlock G, McMillan W, Moore P, Simpson R (2003) Compass: software for computer skills assessment. In: CSUN 2003 international conference on technology and persons with disabilities, Los Angeles, CA

Kop M (2021) EU artificial intelligence act: the European approach to AI. Stanford-Vienna Transatlantic Technology Law Forum, Transatlantic Antitrust and IPR Developments, Stanford University, Issue

Korman B (1996) Mediation in Comparative Law. Routledge

Kumar RL, Wang Y, Poongodi T, Imoize AL (Eds.) (2021) Internet of things, artificial intelligence and blockchain technology. Springer, Cham

Łągiewska A (2024) Digital Mediation and Algorithmic Neutrality. Cambridge University Press

Mackie KJ, Mackie K (2013) A handbook of dispute resolution: ADR in action. Routledge

Madyoon N (2021) Virtual hearings in international arbitration: challenges, solutions, and threats to enforcement. Arbitr: Int J Arbitr Mediat Disput Manag 87(4)

McCarthy J, Minsky ML, Rochester N, Shannon CE (1955) A proposal for the Dartmouth summer research project on AI. Artif Intell: Crit Concepts 2:44–53

Menkel-Meadow C (2015) Mediation, arbitration, and alternative dispute resolution (ADR). Int Encycl Soc Behav Sci, Elsevier Ltd

Mühlhoff R (2023) Predictive privacy: collective data protection in the context of artificial intelligence and big data. Big Data Soc 10(1): 20539517231166886

Nedungatt G (2013) The law of Talion: an ancient law of Jurisprudence. Iustitia 4(2):279–298

Nottage L, Teramura N, Tanna J (2024) Lawyers and non-lawyers in international arbitration: discovering diminishing diversity. Loy LA Int'l Comp L Rev 47:139

Pant K, Ahamad MS (2022) Evolution of alternative dispute resolution (ADR): explication in context of Indian Judiciary. ADR Strategies: Navigating Conflict Resolution in the Modern Legal World, 178

Pauna T, Kujala J, Aaltonen K (2024) A collaborative delivery model with multi-party contract for industrial engineering projects. Int J Project Organ Manag 16(3):309–341
Pawełoszek I, Kumar N, Solanki U (2022) Artificial intelligence, digital technologies, and the future of law. Futur Econ Law 2(2):24–33
Potin NMP (2024) The digital revolution: blockchain and artificial intelligence in international arbitration. Rev Conflu: Sci Humanit 005:165–188
Ramírez JGC (2024) Natural language processing advancements: breaking barriers in human-computer interaction. J Artif Intell General Sci (JAIGS) 3(1):31–39
Regulation (EU) 2024/1689 (AI Act); Judiciary of Hong Kong (Technology Court – Operation Manual; VC section); Supreme People's Court (PRC) – English page on AI-empowered modernization. cicc.court.gov.cn+3eur-lex.europa.eu+3eur-lex.europa.eu+3
Salar N (2023) Institutional arbitration versus ad hoc arbitration: determining the right choice. J Legal Affairs Dispute Resolut Eng Constr 15(3): 06523002
Sathiadas JP, Wikramanayake GN (2003) Document management techniques and technologies. 5th International information technology conference, June, pp 40–48
Seth H (2023). Soft-law guidance from arbitral organisations for conducting arbitrations. Available at SSRN4584969.
Sethumadhavan S, Arora N, Ganapathi RB, Demme J, Kaiser GE (2009) Compass: a community-driven parallelization advisor for sequential software. In: 2009 ICSE workshop on multicore software engineering. IEEE, pp 41–48
Sotoudeh MS (2024) Investigating employment of AI arbitrators in International Commercial Arbitration according to UNCITRAL Model Law (1985). SN Soc Sci 4(10)
Susman K (2021) Between the tiles: the psychology of the virtual room. Appropriating and subverting the digital sphere for authentic and meaningful encounter. Person-Cent Exp Psychother 20(4):327–344
Tai MCT (2020) The impact of artificial intelligence on human society and bioethics. Tzu Chi Med J 32(4):339–343
Tu SS, Cyphert A, Perl S (2024) Artificial intelligence: legal reasoning, legal research and legal writing. In: Artificial intelligence: legal reasoning, legal research and legal writing (May 5, 2024). Minn JL Sci & Tech (Forthcoming)
Van Ettekoven BJ, Prins C (2024) Artificial intelligence and the judiciary system. In Research handbook in data science and law. Edward Elgar Publishing, pp 361–387
Wade KA, Cartwright-Finch U (2022) The science of witness memory: implications for practice and procedure in international arbitration. J Int Arbitr 39(1)
Willis T (2025) NEC4: effective preparation and management of the construction programme. Emerald Publishing Limited

Chapter 5
Epilogue

The role of artificial intelligence in shaping the future of arbitration is indisputable. The utilisation of advanced technologies, including machine learning and natural language processing, has the potential to transform the landscape of dispute resolution. The utilisation of artificial intelligence in the domain of arbitration systems holds the promise of enhancing the efficacy of the process through the automation of routine tasks. These tasks encompass the review, analysis, quantification, classification and processing of documentary, expert and testimonial evidence. This, in turn, enables arbitrators to prioritise the evaluation of the case's merits and the resolution of complex issues that emerge during the course of the proceedings.

The utilisation of AI algorithms, through the analysis of substantial data and procedural content from prior cases, facilitates reasoned decision-making by arbitrators. This integration has been demonstrated to reduce time expenditure, whilst concomitantly promoting greater transparency and fairness by mitigating human biases. However, it is important to recognise that although the benefits of AI are undeniable, its implementation requires caution (Neuwirth 2024).

It is imperative that there is harmonisation between human discernment and technological support in order to ensure the credibility of the arbitration process, whilst simultaneously maximising the effectiveness of AI in conflict resolution. A critical aspect of this issue is the need for strict regulation and adequate supervision, with the definition of clear guidelines that guarantee the ethical and responsible use of these systems. Furthermore, continuous monitoring of algorithms is imperative to avert systemic distortions or errors (Arvidsson and Jones (Eds.), 2024).

The adoption of these safeguards will facilitate the utilisation of AI to enhance arbitration processes, while ensuring the preservation of trust and institutional integrity.

The integration of artificial intelligence (AI) and blockchain technology into the conclusion of commercial contracts has the potential to transform contract management.

F. Messias, *The Practice of Law and International Arbitration in the Age of Artificial Intelligence*, SpringerBriefs in Law,
https://doi.org/10.1007/978-3-032-09127-7_5

As smart contracts, supported by AI algorithms, become more sophisticated, the implications for process automation and optimisation increase. The synergy between these technologies has been demonstrated to reinforce reliability, security and transparency in contract management. Furthermore, it has been shown to enable the autonomous and intelligent execution of clauses, thereby marking a transition to more efficient and technologically advanced models.

The integration of these systems has been shown to engender a number of benefits, including enhanced operational efficiency, a reduction in human error, greater security through immutable records, and increased precision in predictive risk analysis. Nevertheless, there remain several technical and legal challenges to be addressed, including the complexity of implementation, the high initial costs, data privacy issues, and the necessity for specific legal frameworks. In order to address these challenges, it is advised that organisations implement a phased approach, specialised training, ongoing audits and strict adherence to regulations such as the General Data Protection Regulation (GDPR).

With regard to pragmatic recommendations, the significance of comprehending the interoperability between AI and blockchain emerges as a salient point. While artificial intelligence has been demonstrated to accelerate the analysis of clauses and the simulation of contractual scenarios, blockchain has been shown to ensure the incorruptible execution of terms, thus creating a reliable automation ecosystem. However, the implementation of smart contracts on platforms such as Ethereum necessitates a meticulous technical evaluation to ensure congruence with the particular requirements of each business operation.

It is imperative that data security is prioritised through the application of advanced encryption techniques, hierarchical access controls and the anonymisation of sensitive information. Concurrently, a diligent approach to the evaluation of technology providers necessitates a comprehensive analysis encompassing their reputation, compliance history, and the robustness of the infrastructures they offer.

Continuous monitoring of the performance of these systems through key performance indicators (e.g. average processing time, automatic execution accuracy rate) allows for iterative adjustments, ensuring adaptability in the face of technological evolution. Periodic revision of algorithms and protocols is also crucial to maintain competitiveness and avoid obsolescence.

To summarise, the convergence of AI and blockchain is an emerging paradigm in contract management, with tangible advantages in terms of efficiency and security. However, its adoption requires a strategic balance between innovation and caution, ensuring that technological advances do not jeopardise legal compliance or the protection of the parties involved. The future evolution of these technologies will tend to consolidate their use, as long as it is accompanied by clear regulatory frameworks and responsible business practices. Emerging perspectives on the evolution of AI governance and arbitral practice are discussed across recent scholarship (Arvidsson and Jones 2024; Chan, Bel and Malek 2024; Chan, Gore and Jiang 2023; Chan and Lejiniece 2024; El Amari, Khalaf and Hamam 2024; Gómez-Moreno 2024; Mühlhoff 2023; Ramírez 2024; Soyer and

Tettenborn 2022; Tai 2020; Tu, Cyphert and Perl 2024; Van Ettekoven and Prins 2024).

The impact of AI on legal systems is manifested through technologies such as Natural Language Processing, Machine Learning and decision support systems, which are redefining procedural procedures.

These tools boost efficiency in collecting, transmitting and analysing data, automating repetitive tasks and offering detailed predictive assessments. However, their adoption entails structural risks: the replacement of traditional functions, the erosion of human analytical skills and the propagation of algorithmic biases in judicial or arbitration decisions.

Mitigating these risks requires a robust ethical framework based on operational transparency, periodic technical audits and AI models capable of critical self-regulation. In this context, it is proposed that specialised functions be institutionalised: the Responsible for the Legal Supervision of AI (RSJIA), tasked with monitoring technological compliance with legal principles; the Responsible for the Legal Compliance of AI (RCJIA), focused on alignment with sectoral regulations; and the Responsible for the Legal Quality of AI (RQJIA), guaranteeing technical precision and the absence of systemic discrimination.

In international arbitration, digitalisation introduces paradigmatic challenges. The virtualisation of hearings—although speedy—raises questions about the authenticity of evidence, particularly in the production of testimonial evidence. The absence of physical presence requires adaptations in procedural dynamics, with reinforcement of protocols for verifying identity and document integrity (Anderson and Verbist (Eds.), 2024). At the same time, opportunities are emerging: automated file management, predictive analysis of contractual risks and optimisation of oral proceedings through collaborative platforms.

The convergence of innovation and legal tradition requires a delicate balance. Continuing education for judicial operators is imperative to preserve essential skills in the face of increasing automation. Longitudinal studies are needed to assess the socio-professional impact of AI, while interdisciplinary co-operation (lawyers, engineers, ethicists) should guide the development of inclusive and auditable tools.

To summarise, AI is a catalyst for efficiency, but its implementation lacks epistemological safeguards.

Maintaining the principles of equity and material justice requires not only adaptive regulation, but also a proactive redefinition of human roles in the legal ecosystem. The future of law will depend on the ability to harmonise algorithms with legal axiology, ensuring that technological progress does not eclipse the ethical foundations of legal practice.

The integration of digital technologies into international arbitration redefines procedural paradigms, requiring structural adaptations in the conduct of hearings and evidentiary management. The transition to remote formats requires a reassessment of traditional dynamics, such as the interpretation of non-verbal language in virtual environments, which loses critical nuances in the face of digital mediation. To mitigate this impact, it is imperative to establish clear protocols regulating remote participation, ensuring procedural fairness and preserving the integrity of testimonial evidence. These guidelines should include specific training for arbitrators in virtual moderation techniques, standardisation of technical requirements (e.g. transmission quality, biometric authentication) and the adoption of safeguards against technological interruptions.

The credibility of witnesses in digital environments depends on the implementation of mechanisms that reinforce transparency, such as the full recording of sessions with blockchain timestamps and the use of AI to detect narrative inconsistencies. However, this approach requires caution to avoid the erosion of adversarial proceedings, ensuring that the parties retain full capacity to question and re-analyse the evidence. The combination of AI analytical tools and secure document sharing platforms can optimise efficiency, provided they are aligned with ethical principles and regulations such as the GDPR.

Resource allocation emerges as a central challenge: digitalisation requires investment in technical infrastructure and specialised training, creating asymmetries between parties with different economic capacities. To neutralise this risk, it is proposed to create transnational support funds, managed by arbitral institutions, to subsidise equipment and connectivity for developing countries. At the same time, testing prior to hearings—including simulations of technical failure scenarios—has become an indispensable practice to ensure procedural fluidity.

The digital transformation in international arbitration is not a mere virtual replication of face-to-face models, but a profound re-engineering of legal communication. This evolution requires the redefinition of professional skills, with an emphasis on digital literacy, the management of collaborative platforms and the critical interpretation of algorithmic data. Future research should focus on objectively quantifying the cognitive impact of virtualisation—for example, through comparative studies on conviction rates in face-to-face versus remote formats—and on developing interoperable frameworks for cross-validating electronic evidence.

The sustainability of this transition depends on harmonising innovation and tradition. While AI and blockchain offer solutions for authentication and efficiency, their implementation must safeguard established procedural guarantees, such as the right to secrecy of justice and technological privacy. Co-operation between regulators, technology providers and legal communities is crucial to establishing universal standards, avoiding regulatory fragmentation. In this context, international arbitration can be positioned as a privileged laboratory for the experimental governance of emerging technologies, provided it is anchored in principles of equal access, algorithmic transparency and ethical responsibility. Recent scholarship (Arvidsson and Jones 2024; Chan et al 2024; Gómez-Moreno 2024; Mühlhoff 2023) anticipates the convergence of AI governance and arbitration practice.

The absence of explicit references to remote hearings in national arbitration laws constitutes a relevant regulatory gap, although arbitral institutions have made progress in revising their regulations, integrating specific provisions for virtual proceedings. Such adaptations, resulting from the disruptive impact of digital technologies on legal semiotics, reflect good practices to be consolidated, particularly with regard to the interactive presentation of evidence or witness production in a remote environment—areas that require in-depth research.

The inherent complexity of multi-party and multi-jurisdictional arbitrations necessitates the implementation of robust technological solutions. Such solutions must be capable of ensuring procedural fairness, expediency, and evidentiary integrity. The implementation of digital tools in these scenarios necessitates cross-border verification mechanisms, platform interoperability, and guarantees of equal access to technical resources, particularly for parties from jurisdictions with limited infrastructures. Collaboration between arbitration centres, academics and technology developers is crucial to creating unified protocols, thereby mitigating the risk of regulatory fragmentation.

Within the domain of Online Dispute Resolution (ODR), the integration of artificial intelligence (AI) introduces a series of paradoxes. While AI enhances the efficiency of data analysis and outcome prediction, its capacity for self-regulation is incongruent with the tenets of transparency and adversarialism that underpin the ODR framework. The absence of specific legal frameworks for AI in ODR, at national, European or international level, serves to exacerbate the risks of procedural dehumanisation. It is therefore imperative to develop a European Model Law that establishes ethical limits to automation, ensuring human supervision by certified entities and harmonising accountability standards.

The future of international arbitration and ODR will depend on the ability to balance innovation with epistemological safeguards. It is imperative that there is continuous monitoring of algorithms, specialised training for arbitrators in digital literacy, and the establishment of technological support funds for developing countries. Concurrently, research should prioritise empirical studies on the cognitive impact of remote hearings and the legal validation of AI-generated evidence, thereby ensuring that technical advances do not compromise historical procedural guarantees (Soyer (Ed.), 2024).

It is asserted that proactive regulation, in combination with transdisciplinary cooperation, will facilitate the transformation of digital challenges into opportunities, while ensuring the preservation of the fundamental principles of arbitration: efficiency, fairness and material justice. The sustainability of this transition requires not only regulatory adaptation, but also an ethical redefinition of the role of technology in access to justice.

References

Anderson A, Verbist H (Eds) (2024) Expedited International Arbitration: policies, Rules, and Procedures. Kluwer Law International BV

Arvidsson M, Jones E (Eds) (2024) International Law and Posthuman Theory. Taylor & Francis

Chan E, Bel MG, Malek B (2024) SVAMC Draft Guidelines on Using AI in Arbitration: a Focus on the Selection of Arbitrators and Arbitrators' Use of AI. NY Disp Resol Law 12

Chan E, Lejniece A (2024) The Technological Competence of Arbitrators: a Comparative and International Legal Study

Chan E, Gore KN, Jiang E (2023) Harnessing Artificial Intelligence in International Arbitration Practice. Contemp Asia Arbitr J 16:263

El Amari M, Khalaf OI, Hamam H (2024) AI-Driven Solutions in Healthcare, Education, and Legal Systems (No. 12530). EasyChair

Gómez-Moreno JP (2024) Advocacy for Online Proceedings: features of the Digital World and Their Role in How Communication is Shaped in Remote International Arbitration. International Journal for the Semiotics of Law-Revue Internationale de Sémiotique Juridique 37(3):865–885

Mühlhoff R (2023) Predictive privacy: collective data protection in the context of artificial intelligence and big data. Big Data and Society 10(1):20539517231166886

Neuwirth RJ (2024) Law, artificial intelligence, and synaesthesia. AI and Society 39(3):901–912

Ramírez JGC (2024) Natural Language Processing Advancements: breaking Barriers in Human-Computer Interaction. J Artiff Intel Gen Sci (JAIGS) 3(1):31–39

Soyer B (Ed) (2024) Commercial Disputes: resolution and Jurisdiction. Taylor & Francis

Soyer B, Tettenborn A (2022) Artificial intelligence and civil liability—do we need a new regime? Int J Law Inf Technol 30(4):385–397

Tai MCT (2020) The impact of artificial intelligence on human society and bioethics. Tzu Chi Med J 32(4):339–343

Tu SS, Cyphert A, Perl S (2024) Artificial Intelligence: legal Reasoning, Legal Research and Legal Writing. In: Artificial Intelligence: legal Reasoning, Legal Research and Legal Writing (May 5, 2024). Minn JL Sci & Tech (Forthcoming)

Van Ettekoven BJ, Prins C (2024) Artificial intelligence and the judiciary system. In: Research Handbook in Data Science and Law. Edward Elgar Publishing, pp 361–387

Appendix: Publications

Law & Business

Messias, F. (2013). Company Law Analysis and Leadership in Risk Taking—The Portuguese Company Scenario. Allahabad, India: Rochak Publishing.

Messias, F. (2013). Corporate Governance and Corporate Lawyers—Company Laws in Portugal and Risk Analysis. Allahabad, India: Rochak Publishing.

Messias, F. (2013). Corporate Social Responsibility—Is Your Company in Portugal on the Right Track? Allahabad, India: Rochak Publishing.

Messias, F. (2013). Leadership & Management Litigation Risk—A Mental Model Methodology to Reduce the Risk of Claims for Damage to the Company Following "Bad" Business Decisions: The Portuguese Company Scenario. Allahabad, India: Rochak Publishing.

Messias, F. (2013). Novas perspectivas na responsabilidade do Estado—O impacto da liderança organizacional no bem-estar dos trabalhadores. Allahabad, India: Rochak Publishing.

Messias, F. (2013). Portugal—Analysis of the Company Laws and Corporate Social Responsibility: Does Leadership and Employee Well-Being Matter? Allahabad, India: Rochak Publishing.

Messias, F. (2015). Bien-être organisationnel dans l'Hôtellerie Cinq étoiles: Le rôle du leadership promoteur de bienêtre. Allahabad, Índia: Rochak Publishing.

F. Messias, *The Practice of Law and International Arbitration in the Age of Artificial Intelligence*, SpringerBriefs in Law,
https://doi.org/10.1007/978-3-032-09127-7

Messias, F. (2015). O Bem-Estar Organizacional na Hotelaria de Cinco Estrelas: O papel da Liderança Promotora de Bem-Estar. Allahabad, India: Rochak Publishing.

Messias, F. (2015). The Organizational Well-Being in Five-Star Hospitality: The Role of Leadership Which Promotes Well-Being. Allahabad, India: Rochak Publishing.

Messias, F. (2020). Liderança organizacional: conceitos e principais teorias. Allahabad, India: Rochak Publishing.

Messias, F. (2025). A prática do Direito e da Arbitragem Internacional na Era da Inteligência Artificial. Allahabad, India: Rochak Publishing.

Chapters

Law & Business

Messias, F. (2011). Portugal—Analysis of the Company Laws. In W. H. Byrnes (Ed.), International Trust Laws and Analysis: Company Laws, Wealth Management & Tax Planning Strategies. Kluwer Law International.

Messias, F. (2017). Portugal—Analysis of the Company Laws. In W. H. Byrnes (Ed.), International Trust Laws and Analysis: Company Laws, Wealth Management & Tax Planning Strategies. Kluwer Law International.

Messias, F. (2020). Portugal—Analysis of the Company Laws. In W. H. Byrnes (Ed.), International Trust Laws and Analysis: Company Laws, Wealth Management & Tax Planning Strategies. Kluwer Law International.

Fiction & Essay

Heine, E. (2014). A Passagem. Allahabad, India: Cyberwit.net.

Heine, E. (2014). Le Passage. Allahabad, India: Cyberwit.net.

Heine, E. (2015). O Ventre e o Medo. Allahabad, India: Cyberwit.net.

Heine, E. (2016). Le ventre et la peur. Allahabad, India: Cyberwit.net.

Johakin, S. (2014). Deux rêves. Allahabad, India: Cyberwit.net.

Johakin, S. (2014). Dois Sonhos. Allahabad, India: Cyberwit.net.

Johakin, S. (2016). Le Regard de Dieu. Allahabad, India: Cyberwit.net.

Johakin, S. (2016). O Olhar de Deus. Allahabad, India: Cyberwit.net.

Messias, F. (2013). Cristóvão Colon e a Descoberta da América—Poesia Selecionada a Cristóvão Colon. Allahabad, Índia: Cyberwit.net.

Messias, F. (2013). Doutrina da Palavra—Construção. Allahabad, Índia: Cyberwit.net.

Messias, F. (2013). Doutrina da Palavra—Desconstrução. Allahabad, Índia: Cyberwit.net.

Messias, F. (2013). Doutrina da Palavra—Movimento. Allahabad, Índia: Cyberwit.net.

Messias, F. (2013). The Hidden Truth of the Discovery of America: The Mystery of Columbus—Selected Poetry to Cristóvão Colon. Allahabad, Índia: Cyberwit.net.

Messias, F. (2015). A viagem do sol na constelação do grande poema. Allahabad, Índia: Cyberwit.net.

Messias, F. (2015). O Sopro da Palavra—As cinquenta cores de um movimento perpétuo. Allahabad, Índia: Cyberwit.net.

Messias, F. (2015). Pensamentos Visionados. Allahabad, Índia: Cyberwit.net.

Messias, F. (2016). Le souffle du mot—Les cinquante couleurs d'un mouvement perpétuel. Allahabad, Índia: Cyberwit.net.

Messias, F. (2016). Pensées Visionnées. Allahabad, Índia: Cyberwit.net.

Messias, F. (2024). O Rei e a Rainha—O Palácio Arehns. Vila Nova de Famalicão: Editorial Novembro.

Messias, F. (2025). Advocacia e Bem-Estar. Santo Tirso: Editorial Novembro.

Messias, F., & Sousa, A. (2020). Human—o oito, o tudo, e o nada: reflexões de universalidade, equilíbrio e intemporalidade. Allahabad, Índia: Cyberwit.net.

Sabóia, A. (2015). Abandonment. Allahabad, Índia: Cyberwit.net.

Stolkin, E. (2015). O Rei e a Rainha—O Palácio Arehns. Allahabad, Índia: Cyberwit.net.

Articles

Messias, F. (2016). Comportamentos do líder promotor de bem-estar na hotelaria de cinco estrelas. In Proceedings of the International Congress on Interdisciplinary in Social and Human Sciences, Universidade do Algarve.

Messias, F. (2024). A parentalidade e a regulação das responsabilidades parentais: os pais no papel de líderes promotores de bem-estar. In F. Bayle (Ed.), Distúrbios da Parentalidade II. Editorial Novembro.

Messias, F. (2025). Dispute resolution and prevention: Europe, Morocco, and Saudi Arabia—Venues for the 2030 and 2034 FIFA World Cup. Paper presented at Seminar on Dispute Resolution and Prevention, ICAM, Madrid.

Messias, F. (2025). International arbitration in the age of artificial intelligence. In White Book Developments on International Arbitration 2025: Future is Now. IIMAT.

Messias, F. B. (2016). A importância da liderança na hotelaria de cinco estrelas. Publituris, 1314, 30.

Messias, F., Mendes, J., & Monteiro, I. (2010). The effects of leadership behaviors on the employee well-being in the workplace: A worthy investment from managers or leaders. In Proceedings of the 6th International Symposium on Entrepreneurship in Tourism (pp. 141–159). Universidade do Algarve.

Messias, F., Mendes, J., & Monteiro, I. (2011). Leadership and well-being in the Algarve hospitality. In J. S. Santos, F. Perdigão, P. Águas, & K. Torkington (Eds.), Book of Proceedings of the International Conference on Tourism & Management Studies, Special Issue (Vol. II, pp. 1060–1062).

Messias, F., Mendes, J., & Monteiro, I. (2011). Leadership and well-being in hospitality industry, new challenges. In Conference on Modern Hospitality and Tourism Development, Allmed University, Teerão, Irão.

Messias, F., Mendes, J., & Monteiro, I. (2011). Liderança e bem-estar na hotelaria no Algarve. In First International Conference on Tourism and Management Studies, Universidade do Algarve.

Messias, F., Mendes, J., & Monteiro, I. (2013). O impacto da liderança no bem-estar dos colaboradores—O papel dos líderes e dos gestores na construção de modelos que promovam o bem-estar psicológico no trabalho. Dos Algarves: A Multidisciplinary e-Journal, 22, 59–75.

Participation in Academic Examination Boards

Doctoral Thesis Jury

Member of the jury for the thesis 'Satisfaction of hotel professionals—study of the relationships with personal and organisational variables' by Sérgio Jorge Pereira Da Borralha, as part of a PhD in Psychology at the Faculty of Psychology, University of Algarve (2018).

Master's Dissertation Jury

Member of the jury for the thesis 'Geoeconomics of the Portuguese Continental Shelf: Cruise Tourism' by José Gregório Gustavo Rodriguez Gonçalves, as part of the Master's Degree in Land Management—Remote Sensing and Geographic Information Systems, at the Faculty of Social and Human Sciences of the New University of Lisbon (2019).

MIX
Papier aus verantwortungsvollen Quellen
Paper from responsible sources
FSC® C105338

If you have any concerns about our products,
you can contact us on
ProductSafety@springernature.com

In case Publisher is established outside the EU,
the EU authorized representative is:
Springer Nature Customer Service Center GmbH
Europaplatz 3, 69115 Heidelberg, Germany

Printed by Libri Plureos GmbH
in Hamburg, Germany